ROCKY MOUNTAIN
NATIONAL PARK
THE COMPLETE GUIDE

1st Edition

©2021 DESTINATION PRESS & ITS LICENSORS
ISBN: 9781940754475

Written, Photographed, and Illustrated
by James Kaiser

A very special thanks to all National Park Service employees who helped with this book, particularly Katy Sykes, who offered invaluable input. A big thanks to Kyle Patterson, Kelly Cahill, Sybil Barnes, John Meissner, and Karl Kahler. Lon Abbott and Joanna Lambert at the University of Colorado Boulder offered terrific insights into geology and ecology. Thanks also to Maria Sears, Emily Sears, Eric Reinhardt, Kevin Whitcher, Susan Smith, Bella Singh, Jason Van Taterhoven, and the Estes Park writers group.

Thanks to my family, friends, and all those who supported me while working on this book (particularly Jeff Eldridge of Liberty Puzzles who sheltered the Kaisers during the 2020 wildfires!). And a very special thanks to my wonderful wife Andrea Rincon and our baby girl Martina, who accompanied me on many adventures in the park.

All information in this guide has been exhaustively researched and all maps are based on USGS data, but information does change. If you encounter a change or mistake while using this guide, please email changes@jameskaiser.com. Your input will help make future editions even better.

Additional image and photography credits listed on individual pages.
Printed in Malaysia

ROCKY MOUNTAIN

NATIONAL PARK

THE COMPLETE GUIDE

1st Edition

JAMES KAISER

CONGRATULATIONS!

IF YOU'VE PURCHASED this book, you're going to Rocky Mountain National Park. Perhaps you're already here. If so, you're in one of the most beautiful places in America—a rugged alpine landscape filled with dramatic geology and world-class outdoor adventures.

Colorado is famous for mountains, but few places in the state are as captivating as Rocky Mountain National Park. Straddling the Continental Divide, the park's lofty peaks tower above some of the southernmost glaciers in the Rockies. In spring, melting snow tumbles down deep canyons and feeds pristine lakes and sparkling waterfalls. Colorful wildflowers blanket alpine meadows in summer, while shimmering aspen trees light up hillsides in autumn. Abundant wildlife roams the park year-round. Towering above the rugged landscape is 14,259-foot Longs Peak, the tallest summit in the park and Colorado's most iconic fourteener.

But Rocky Mountain National Park is much more than just pretty views. When I first visited the park, I was awed by the scenery. The more I learned, the more I realized it's also one of America's most remarkable outdoor classrooms. Ancient volcanoes, Ice Age glaciers, vast alpine tundra, rich native history, rugged pioneers, magnificent wildlife—the landscape is bursting with fascinating stories. And yet many visitors drive through the park unaware of the astonishing world surrounding them.

That's where this book comes in. Whether you're climbing rugged mountains or going for a leisurely drive along Trail Ridge Road, *Rocky Mountain National Park: The Complete Guide* reveals the hidden stories of this extraordinary corner of the Rockies. From outdoor adventures to ancient geology, alpine ecology to abandoned ghost towns, my book puts the best of the park at your fingertips.

So strap on your hiking boots and grab some sunscreen. It's time to explore Rocky Mountain National Park!

CONTENTS

ADVENTURES 15

Hiking, backpacking, rock climbing, fly fishing, horseback riding—Rocky is filled with outdoor adventures. The only question is what not to do in the park!

BASICS 32 & GATEWAY TOWNS 47

Everything you need to know, from gateway towns to park fees to seasonal weather patterns. Whatever your plans, arrive prepared to make the most of your time in Rocky.

GEOLOGY 57

Learn about the powerful forces that shaped the Rockies. Nearly two billion years of earth history created one of America's most beautiful landscapes.

ECOLOGY & WILDLIFE 69

The park shelters an incredible range of plants and animals—from delicate wildflowers to enormous elk. Discover Rocky's amazing ecology, from meadows to mountaintops.

HISTORY 105

For over 10,000 years, prehistoric cultures and modern tribes lived in northern Colorado. The region was settled by Europeans following the discovery of gold in the mid-1800s, and a colorful cast of characters gathered in Estes Park. By the early 1900s, citizens united to create Rocky Mountain National Park. Over the past century this exquisite alpine land-scape has attracted millions of adventurers from around the world.

MORAINE PARK 133
& BEAR LAKE 149

The park's most popular region is filled with stunning lakes and gorgeous meadows—all surrounded by the majestic peaks of the Front Range.

LONGS PEAK & WILD BASIN 177

Longs Peak is the tallest mountain in the park and one of Colorado's top adventures. Wild Basin boasts some of the park's best hiking trails.

LUMPY RIDGE 211

Towering over Estes Park, Lumpy Ridge's unusual granite formations lure hikers and rock climbers.

FALL RIVER 219 & TRAIL RIDGE ROAD 237

Fall River showcases some of the best glacial geology in the park. Trail Ridge Road rises over 12,000 feet above sea level, offering stunning views from the top of the Rockies.

KAWUNEECHE VALLEY 273

Sculpted by the park's largest glacier, Kawuneeche Valley reveals gorgeous scenery west of the Continental Divide.

ROCKY TOP 5

TOP 5 VIEWS

Alpine Visitor Center, 259
Rainbow Curve, 243
Forest Canyon Overlook, 246
Gore Range Overlook, 257
Longs Peak, 196

TOP 5 WATERFALLS

Alberta Falls, 164
Chasm Falls, 228
Adams Falls, 280
Ouzel Falls, 188
Calypso Cascades, 191

TOP 5 EASY HIKES

Tundra Communities Trail, 250
Bear Lake, 157
Sprague Lake, 155
Alluvial Fan, 227
Coyote Valley, 278

TOP 5 HARD HIKES

Chasm Lake, 194
Sky Pond, 168
Flattop Mountain, 172
Twin Sisters, 184
Lake Verna, 286

Sprague Lake

INTRODUCTION

STRADDLING THE CONTINENTAL DIVIDE in northern Colorado, Rocky Mountain National Park boasts the highest average elevation of any U.S. national park. Over one hundred 11,000-foot peaks lie within its boundaries, towering over forests dotted with lush meadows and shimmering lakes. Twisting through the heart of this alpine wonderland is Trail Ridge Road, the highest continuous road in America, which rises above treeline and passes through a dazzling expanse of alpine tundra.

Over 350 miles of hiking trails crisscross the park, ranging from easy strolls to rugged scrambles up the highest peaks. The park's tallest mountain, 14,259-foot Longs Peak, is one of Colorado's most famous landmarks, and the challenging route to its summit is one of the state's top adventures. Rock climbers test their mettle on Long Peak's sheer eastern face—one of the most formidable big walls in North America.

Abundant wildlife roams the park's 415 square miles, including elk, deer, moose, and bighorn sheep. During the autumn elk rut, the haunting bugle of dominant bulls echoes through the park's glacially carved canyons. Venture to the park's highest elevations and you'll find fascinating animals well-adapted to the harsh environment. Marmots and pikas scurry among the rocks, while white-tailed ptarmigans—one of over 270 bird species in the park—blend into alpine tundra using exceptional camouflage.

Most visitors enter Rocky Mountain National Park from Estes Park, a small mountain town just east of the park. Nestled in a gorgeous valley, Estes Park boasts scenery worthy of its own national park. Its historic downtown bustles with tourists, and dozens of hotels and lodges dot the outskirts of town. The park's only western entrance is located next to Grand Lake, the largest natural body of water in Colorado.

Humans have occupied this majestic region for thousands of years. Ancient hunters ventured above treeline in search of prey, and both the Utes and Arapahoes spent time in the park. Following the Colorado Gold Rush, European immigrants settled the land. By the start of the 20th century, there was a growing movement to protect the landscape. Local naturalist Enos Mills dedicated his life to the creation of Rocky Mountain National Park, which was established in 1915. For over a century "Rocky" has protected one of the most beautiful locations in Colorado. Today it attracts over four million visitors each year.

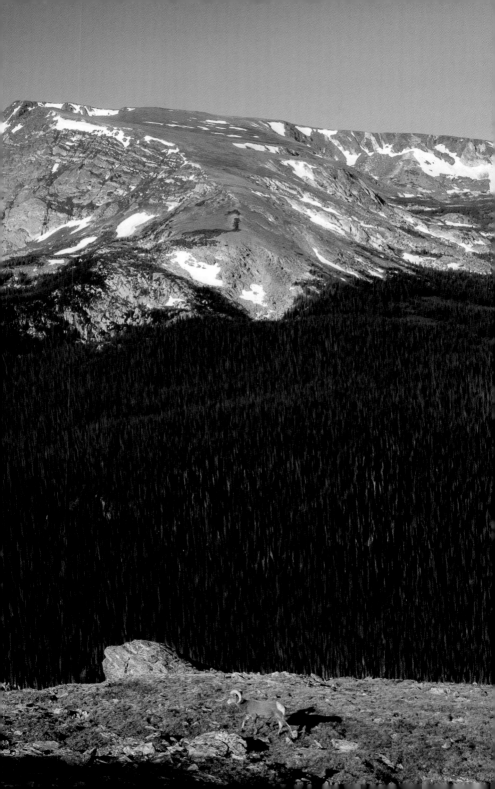

HIKING

Hiking is one of the best ways to experience Rocky Mountain National Park. Nothing brings you closer to the gorgeous scenery than stepping out of your car and strolling through the mountains. There are hiking trails for every age and ability, many of which lead to spectacular waterfalls, lakes, and summits that can only be reached on foot. This guidebook provides maps and logistics for over two dozen of the park's best hikes.

Rocky Mountain National Park boasts over 350 miles of hiking trails. The most popular trails are concentrated in three major areas: Bear Lake (p.149), Wild Basin (p.177), and Kawuneeche Valley (p.273). Other great hiking areas include Moraine Park (p.133), Lumpy Ridge (p.211), and Fall River (p.219). Day hikers do not need permits on established trails. Backpackers camping in the wilderness require permits to spend the night in the park.

The park's hiking season gears up in spring, when winter snowpack starts to melt. As the months progress, temperatures creep higher and higher, and by late June nearly all trails are snow-free. Be aware that conditions can vary considerably from year to year. Following winters with particularly heavy snow, Rocky's highest trails can retain snow until July.

Always check current conditions before hitting the trail. The park's website (nps.gov/romo) lists current trail conditions, and the knowledgeable staff at Wilderness Offices (p.20) can answer questions and provide guidance for trails throughout the park. Serious hikers should also purchase a detailed topographic map. My favorite map is National Geographic's *Trails Illustrated Rocky Mountain National Park*.

Balmy summer temperatures lure thousands of hikers to the park. But July and August are also monsoon season, when afternoon thunderstorms roll through the mountains on an almost daily basis (p.42). Always aim for an early start in summer. You'll beat the crowds *and* avoid afternoon thunderstorms. September is one of the park's best hiking months, with mild sunny days and glorious foliage towards the end of the month. Depending on snowfall, the park's hiking season can sometimes stretch into November. And with the right gear and proper training, you can even hike in winter.

What to Pack

While hiking, it's best to dress in layers, adding or removing clothes to maximize comfort. Quick-drying synthetic fabrics or merino wool are better than cotton, which retains moisture. Always pack a rain jacket, which also functions as a windbreaker. Ultraviolet rays are stronger at higher elevations, so use sunglasses, sunscreen, and a wide-brimmed hat. Temperatures can drop rapidly—always pack warm clothes and a warm hat. Colorado has a famously dry climate, and it's easy to become dehydrated at high elevations, so bring plenty of water (two liters or more for longer hikes). Salty snacks are also essential when you're sweating. Hiking poles take pressure off your knees and increase stability, particularly while descending steep trails. Insect repellent with DEET helps keep mosquitoes and ticks away. A map and compass are essential, and always pack a headlamp in case you don't return before dark.

Hazards

Many of the park's hazards—altitude sickness, lightning, wildlife, ticks, giardiasis—are magnified while hiking. See page 36 for a discussion of these hazards. Lightning is of particular concern for anyone climbing exposed peaks. Thunderstorms can develop quickly, so always scan the horizon for dark clouds. During monsoon season, aim to be below treeline before afternoon thunderstorms arrive. Many forests are filled with dead trees killed by bark beetles; be aware of the potential for falling trees. During the colder months, when snow and ice cover many trails, it's a good idea to bring microspikes that attach to hiking boots, giving you better traction. Avalanches are also a hazard during the cold, snowy winter months.

Leave No Trace

While visiting Rocky Mountain National Park, always follow the Leave No Trace Seven Principles: plan ahead and prepare, travel and camp on durable surfaces, dispose of waste properly, leave what you find, minimize campfire impacts, respect wildlife, and be considerate of other visitors. Learn more at lnt.org.

Dogs & Pets

Dogs and other pets are not allowed on any park trails.

Guided Hikes

If you prefer hiking with a professional, both Rocky Mountain Conservancy Field Institute (p.32) and the Colorado Mountain School (p.36) offer guided hikes in Rocky Mountain National Park.

Rocky's Best Hikes

Emerald Lake

Ouzel Falls

Lake Verna

BACKPACKING

ROCKY MOUNTAIN NATIONAL PARK is a hiking paradise, but backpacking and camping in the wilderness takes hiking to a whole new level. When day hikers are heading home, backpackers are relaxing at camp, luxuriating in the park's epic scenery with no crowds. After a long day on the trail, there's nothing like falling asleep under billions of twinkling stars, then waking up to alpine sunshine illuminating pristine wilderness.

Of course, backpacking is more complicated than day hiking. You'll need far more equipment (tent, sleeping bag, water filter, cooking gear, etc.), and you'll need to know how to use it properly. But with great effort comes great reward. If you're new to backpacking, ask about backpacking classes at your local outdoor store. Or contact one of the local outfitters that offers guided backpacking trips in Rocky Mountain National Park (see following page).

Roughly 95% of Rocky Mountain National Park is designated wilderness, and there are over 100 wilderness campsites. Backpackers must stay in designated wilderness campsites, and the park requires permits to minimize impact and reduce crowding. Wilderness permits become available March 1 for camping between May 1 and October 31. Be aware that popular campsites are often booked months in advance. A full description of the permit process is detailed on the following pages.

All hikers in Rocky Mountain National Park must closely monitor the weather, but this is particularly true for backpackers. Afternoon thunderstorms are common in summer, and many campsites are located at high elevations where temperatures can drop below freezing. Before setting out on any backpack, be sure to talk to the knowledgeable staff at park Wilderness Offices. They watch the weather like red-tailed hawks, and they always have the best info on current campsite and trail conditions.

Many wilderness campsites are located along out-and-back trails, often near remote lakes or streams. But there are a handful of terrific, multi-day backpacking loops. One of the most famous is the Continental Divide (p.290), a 26-mile hike that follows a portion of the Continental Divide Trail and passes through alpine tundra along the crest of the Front Range. Another great option is the region between Bear Lake and Moraine Park, where a spiderweb of trails and campsites lets you choose your own multi-day adventure.

Wilderness Campsites

With over 100 wilderness campsites to choose from, selecting one can be overwhelming, particularly for first-time visitors. Many of the recommended hikes in this book have wilderness campsites. If you see a hike that looks good, check out the adjacent map to see if there's a campsite along the trail.

The park's website is the best source of information for wilderness campsites. There's a downloadable PDF map showing every wilderness campsite in the park, plus detailed descriptions of each campsite, including elevation, nearby water sources, and 20-year averages of snow-free dates. Be aware that no more than seven people can camp at one individual campsite, no more than 12 people can camp at a group campsite, and the park does not allow camping more than three consecutive nights at any one campsite.

Wilderness Permits

Wilderness permits are required for all overnight backpacks in Rocky Mountain National Park. Permits become available March 1 at 8am MST for dates between May 1 and October 31. You can request permits online (nps.gov/romo) or in-person at park Wilderness Offices (see below). Many wilderness campsites are reserved months in advance, but last-minute permits are available at Wilderness Offices year-round.

When applying for permits, have the following info handy: wilderness campsite name and number, trailhead in, trailhead out, preferred camping dates (including alternate dates), and vehicle license plate. For wilderness permits issued between May and October there's a $30 fee. There is no fee for wilderness permits issued between November and April. Backpackers can camp in park wilderness a maximum of 21 days each year: seven nights from June through September, 14 nights from October through May.

You can pick up permits at wilderness centers up to 30 days before your trip. You will receive a tent tag to display on your backpack while hiking to your campsite; the tent tag must then be attached to your tent. You will also receive a dash tag to display on the dashboard of your vehicle while parked at the trailhead. Permits not picked up by noon on the first day of your trip will be canceled unless you call before noon to announce a late arrival. If you pick up a permit but decide to cancel your trip, please let the park know! When emergencies such as wildfires happen, the park sends search parties looking for wilderness campers. If you're not on the trail, they'll waste precious time and resources looking for you.

Wilderness Offices

There are two Wilderness Offices in the park: near Beaver Meadows Visitor Center (p.133), and at Kawuneeche Visitor Center (p.279). Call the Wilderness Office at 970-586-1242.

Food Storage

Black bears and other wildlife are drawn to food, garbage, and scented items. While wilderness camping from April through October, you must store all food, garbage, and scented items in bear-resistant canisters. Place canisters 70 adult steps away from campsites. You can bring your own canister or rent one at Estes Park Mountain Shop (estesparkmountainshop.com) or Rocky Mountain Connection (rmconnection.com).

Water Treatment

All wilderness campsites are located near natural water sources. Giardia is common in natural water sources throughout the park (p.37), so all water must be purified before drinking. Purify water using one of the following methods: a giardia-rated filter, boiling water for one minute while adding one additional minute for each 1,000 feet above sea level, purifying tablets, or a UV water purifier.

Campfires

Forests in Rocky Mountain National Park are filled with dead trees (p.77). Wildfires are a serious threat, so fires are only allowed in a handful of designated wilderness campsites with metal fire rings.

Garbage & Human Waste

Backpackers must pack all garbage out of the wilderness. Pit toilets are available at some wilderness campsites. When pit toilets are not available, dig a hole six inches deep at least 200 feet from campsites, water sources, or trails. You must pack out all toilet paper and feminine sanitary products.

Guided Trips

If you feel overwhelmed by all the permits and rules, consider a guided backpacking trip. Private outfitters will handle all of the details, including permits, gear, and food. Kirks Mountain Adventures (kirksmountainadventures.com, 970-577-0790) and Wildland Trekking (wildlandtrekking.com, 800-715-4453) offer guided backpacking trips in the park.

Cross-Country Zones (No Trails)

There are over 20 Wilderness Technical Orienteering Cross Country Zones in the park with no trails or established campsites. Advanced backpackers with strong wilderness skills may travel in these zones. To learn more about rules and regulations in Wilderness Technical Orienteering Cross Country Zones, visit the park's website.

FISHING

COLORADO'S RIVERS AND LAKES lure anglers from around the world, and few places are prettier to fish than Rocky Mountain National Park. There are nearly 50 fishing lakes within the park, many nestled directly below snow-capped peaks. Dozens of streams tumble down the park's mountains, coalescing into a handful of rivers that exit the park and flow through rugged canyons boasting some of the best fly fishing in Colorado.

Trout are common in the Front Range, but just two trout species are native to the park: greenback cutthroat trout and Colorado River cutthroat trout. Greenback cutthroat trout, a species once thought to be extinct, were rediscovered in the 1950s and reintroduced to park lakes. Waters east of the Continental Divide contain greenback cutthroat, while waters west of the divide contain Colorado River cutthroat trout. Non-native fish include brown trout, brook trout, and rainbow trout. Other species include western longnose suckers, western white suckers, and Colorado speckled dace.

The east side of Rocky Mountain National Park has the most fishing lakes, including many that are easy to reach, which makes the east side the park's most popular fishing area. The west side has fewer visitors, and its lakes are often harder to reach, which attracts anglers who prefer remote lakes with less fishing pressure. Float tubes and non-motorized watercraft are allowed on all lakes in the park except Bear Lake. Although it's possible to fish year-round, summer and fall are the most popular fishing seasons.

A Colorado fishing license is required for anyone 16 or older to fish in the park. Fishing licenses are available at stores outside the park or on the Colorado Parks and Wildlife website (cpw.state.co.us). Bait fishing is not allowed, except for children under 12 in waters that are not catch-and-release. The park's website lists additional rules and regulations, including closed waters, catch-and-keep waters, catch-and-release waters, and catch limits.

If you're new to fly fishing, or looking for a knowledgeable guide, there are several local outfitters in Estes Park, including Kirk's Flyshop (kirksflyshop.com, 970-577-0790) and Estes Angler (estesangler.com, 970-586-2110). Kirk's also operates a fly shop in Grand Lake (kirksflyshopgrandlake.com, 970-627-5021).

HORSEBACK RIDING

HORSES ARE PART of Colorado's heritage, and they remain a fabulous way to explore Rocky Mountain National Park. Roughly 260 miles of trails are open to horses and pack animals. Whether you spend a few hours exploring rivers and meadows on a gentle mare, ride thousands of feet to the Continental Divide, or camp in the backcountry with a packhorse, there's no shortage of equine adventures in the park.

One of the best ways to enjoy horseback riding in Rocky Mountain National Park is to book a ride with Hi Country Stables (sombrero.com, 970-533-8155), which operates two stables in the park, at Moraine Park and Glacier Creek, and they offer guided rides from April through October. Hi Country Stables offers 30-minute rides, one-hour rides, and two-hour rides in the park. Custom tours are also available, including camping trips and journeys across the Continental Divide to Grand Lake. Children age 6 and older are allowed to ride if they are big enough. Advance reservations are recommended.

National Park Gateway Stables (skhorses.com, 970-586-5269), located outside the park near Fall River Visitor Center (p.221), offers two-hour rides to Little Horseshoe Park, four-hour rides to Endovalley, six-hour rides to the top of Deer Mountain, and longer specialty rides. They also offer 10– to 30-minute pony rides for "li'l cowpokes" (kids between 2 and 7). Another great outfitter is Jackson Stables (jacksonstables.com, 970-586-3341), located at the YMCA of the Rockies, just east of the park boundary near Glacier Basin. Jackson Stables offers a wide variety of rides ranging from one hour to a full day, as well as pony rides for kids and hayrides with a campfire and marshmallow roast.

It's also possible to bring your own horse or pack animal. The park allows mules, ponies, llamas, and burros on designated trails. Goats are not allowed because they can transmit diseases to bighorn sheep. Although nearly 75% of park trails are open to horses and pack animals, many popular trails near Bear Lake are off limits. To learn more about bringing your own horse or pack animal, visit the park's website.

ROCK CLIMBING

WITH A NAME like "Rocky," it's no surprise the park is a great place to rock climb. When early mountaineer Frederick Chapin visited in the 1880s, he wrote that "Estes Park, in which are many picturesque scenes, is the natural centre for mountaineering in northern Colorado." Over the next century, modern rock climbers blazed thousands of routes up hundreds of walls and crags. And today a new generation of climbers push the limits of gravity on the park's exceptional vertical terrain.

Lumpy Ridge (p.211), located on the northern edge of Estes Park, is one of the most accessible and popular climbing areas in the park. Over three miles of granite domes and outcrops offer over 500 routes, including excellent crack climbing and great bouldering. Be aware that parts of Lumpy Ridge are off limits to climbers during raptor nesting season (February through July).

With 76 peaks over 12,000 feet in Rocky Mountain National Park, there's no shortage of high-altitude climbs. The most famous and iconic is the sheer eastern face of Longs Peak. Called the Diamond, it rises nearly 1,000 vertical feet and boasts over one million square feet of beautiful granite. The Diamond is comparable to Yosemite's big walls—only it's perched 7,000 feet higher, making it among the highest big walls in North America. With over 70 multi-pitch routes, the Diamond lures climbers from around the world. Thin air and unstable weather make it one of Colorado's most challenging climbs, but when skies are clear it's one of the park's most thrilling adventures.

If you're new to rock climbing, the region around Rocky Mountain National Park is a great place to learn. Colorado Mountain School (coloradomountain-school.com, 720-387-8944) offers a number of rock climbing courses, from beginners' classes to advanced multi-day climbs. Climbing gear is available for purchase or rent at Estes Park Mountain Shop (estesparkmountainshop.com, 970-586-6548). A comprehensive climbing guide is beyond the scope of this book, but there are plenty of great guidebooks for sale at local outdoor shops.

No matter where you climb, remember the words of Enos Mills, the father of Rocky Mountain National Park: "Few experiences can put so much into one's life as to climb a mountain summit, and from among the crags and snows and clouds look down upon the beautiful world below."

WINTER ADVENTURES

ROCKY MOUNTAIN NATIONAL PARK is open year-round, but visitation drops as much as 90% in winter. And yet winter is one of the park's most beautiful seasons. When the peaks and pines are covered in snow, Rocky is transformed into a sparkling alpine wonderland, and there's no shortage of ways to get outdoors and enjoy the snow.

Snowshoeing is one of the park's most popular winter adventures. You can rent snowshoes at outdoor shops in Estes Park or Grand Lake, and park rangers offer guided snowshoe walks on both sides of the park from January through March. Sledders enjoy the gentle slopes at Hidden Valley (p.239), which is the only place in the park where sledding is allowed. Cross-country skiers have a variety of options, including Sprague Lake (p.155) and Trail Ridge Road (p.237). Kawuneeche Valley also offers showshoeing and cross-country skiing, and the Grand Lake Nordic Center is just outside the park (grandlakerecreation.com).

Traditional winter sports are just the tip of the iceberg. Rugged Coloradans, never content to sit at home, engage in all manner of frozen adventures. Backcountry skiers haul themselves up towering peaks and drop down narrow couloirs. Rock climbers swing ice picks to scale frozen waterfalls. And elite mountain climbers summit Longs Peak while training for Everest. (After climbing Longs Peak in winter, famed British climber Doug Scott once quipped: "The Himalayas are a great place to train for Longs Peak.") If this sounds like your frozen cup of tea, contact Colorado Mountain School (coloradomountainschool. com, 720-387-8944) in Estes Park. From avalanche training to ice climbing, you'll find a full range of guided winter adventures.

Some winters are snowier than others, and sometimes heavy snow doesn't fall until late in the season. When snow is low, you can still hike the park's trails. You just need the right equipment. When conditions are icy, hiking poles help maintain your balance, and microspikes (removable metal spikes that attach to the bottom of hiking boots) give you much-needed traction. The park lists winter trail reports and snow depths on its website.

No matter how you enjoy the park, be aware of winter's unique hazards. Colorado suffers more avalanche fatalities than any other state. If you plan on spending time in the backcountry, sign up for an avalanche training course, and always check avalanche forecasts online (avalanche.state.co.us).

Astronomy

Today roughly two-thirds of Americans live in cities and towns with so much light pollution they can no longer see the Milky Way. But here in Rocky Mountain National Park, where the air is clean and light pollution is low, the Milky Way still blazes across the sky at night, revealing the heart of our 200-billion-star galaxy. If you're not looking up at night, you're missing half the show.

Don't know much about astronomy? Park rangers sometimes offer free night sky programs, and the Estes Park Memorial Observatory (angelsabove.org) hosts astronomy events year-round. The highlight of the year is the three-day Rocky Mountain National Park Night Sky Festival, which features astronomy talks during the day and stargazing at night. To help preserve the region's dark skies, both Rocky Mountain National Park and the town of Estes Park have installed outdoor light fixtures to reduce light pollution.

Longs Peak is mentioned in the Jules Verne story *From Earth to the Moon*. Published in 1865, it describes the voyage of a spaceship shot out of giant cannon aimed at the moon. To track the spaceship, scientists build a 280-foot-long telescope on Longs Peak (which Verne mistakenly believed was the highest summit in America). The telescope could "follow the stars from the one horizon to the other during their journey through the heavens."

Long before modern astronomers gazed through telescopes, native tribes developed rich mythologies to explain the cosmos. The Arapahoes call the Big Dipper the Broken Backbone, and it is surrounded by constellations representing mountains, rivers, valleys, creeks, and bear claws. Each month the moon has a different name—February is "frost sparkling in the sun," April is "ice breaking in the river," and October is "falling leaves." The Utes, who lived throughout Colorado's mountains, constructed high-altitude observatories and tracked the phases of the sun and moon.

ROCKY BASICS

Getting to Rocky

Rocky Mountain National Park is located roughly 50 miles northwest of Denver (two-hour drive), 30 miles northwest of Boulder (one-hour drive), 30 miles southwest of Fort Collins (one-hour drive), and 180 miles northeast of Grand Junction (four-hour drive). The closest commercial airport is Denver International Airport (DIA). Estes Park (p.47), the park's most popular gateway town, is located on the park's eastern boundary. Estes Park Shuttle (estesparkshuttle.com) offers transportation from DIA to Estes Park. Grand Lake (p.52) is a small gateway town located along the park's western boundary. Visit jameskaiser.com for detailed driving directions, including points of interest along the way.

Entrance Passes

A one-day automobile pass to Rocky Mountain National Park costs $25 ($15 bicycles and walk-ins, $25 motorcycles), a seven-day pass costs $35, and an annual pass costs $70. My favorite option is the Interagency Annual pass ($80), which gives you unlimited access to all U.S. national parks, national monuments, and federal recreation lands for one year. You can purchase entrance passes at all park entrance stations or on Rocky's website (nps.gov/romo).

In 2020, due to the COVID-19 pandemic, the park implemented a timed entry system from June through mid-October. To enter the park, visitors needed a permit, reserved in advance at recreation.gov, that corresponded to a specified date and a specified entry time (6–8am, 8–10am, etc.). A similar reservation system will likely be implemented moving forward to reduce congestion. Visit the park's website for the latest information on timed entry permits.

Entrance Stations

Beaver Meadows

Located four miles west of downtown Estes Park, Beaver Meadows is the park's most popular entrance station because it's the closest entrance station to park highlights including Moraine Park (p.133), Bear Lake (p.149), and Trail Ridge Road (p.237). Be prepared for long waits in peak season.

Fall River

Located five miles northwest of Estes Park, Fall River Entrance offers access to the Fall River region (p.219) and Trail Ridge Road. This is the park's second-most popular entrance station. Fall River Entrance Station is located a quarter-mile west of Fall River Visitor Center (p.221).

Wild Basin

Located 13 miles south of Estes Park, Wild Basin (p.177) offers access to beautiful hiking trails near the park's southern boundary. During peak season, when congestion is high, the park sometimes limits access to Wild Basin.

Grand Lake

This is the only entrance station located on the west side of the park, offering access to Kawuneeche Valley (p.273) and Trail Ridge Road. It's open year-round, but when Trail Ridge Road is closed the road through Kawuneeche Valley is open for only ten miles. Grand Lake Entrance Station is located 0.4 miles north of Kawuneeche Visitor Center.

Current Information

Entrance stations and visitor centers offer free maps and brochures listing seasonal activities. Rocky's website lists park alerts, and road closures are posted on outdoor signs and sometimes on social media. Live webcams on the park's website show real-time conditions at a range of locations. Weather.gov is a great website for accurate weather forecasts. Rocky's Twitter account (@RockyNPS) is a great resource for up-to-the-minute emergency alerts and road closures.

Getting Around
Park Roads

There are three major roads in the park. Bear Lake Road starts just west of Beaver Meadows Entrance Station, and it provides access to Moraine Park and Bear Lake. During peak season the park often closes Bear Lake Road in late morning/early afternoon to limit congestion. With a little planning, however, it's easy to avoid getting shut out. I discuss the best ways to visit Bear Lake in the Bear Lake chapter (p.149). Bear Lake Road is open and plowed year-round.

Trail Ridge Road is the driving highlight of Rocky Mountain National Park. Rising over 12,000 feet above sea level, including 11 miles above treeline, it crosses the Continental Divide and offers some of the most spectacular panoramas in the park. Trail Ridge Road generally closes from late October to late May/early June due to heavy snow. Learn more in the Trail Ridge Road chapter (p.237)

Old Fall River Road is a rugged dirt road that starts in Horseshoe Park and climbs to Alpine Visitor Center next to Trail Ridge Road. It was the first road in Rocky Mountain National Park to cross the Continental Divide, and it was later overshadowed by Trail Ridge Road, but it still makes a delightful drive. Old Fall River Road is generally open July through September, depending on winter snowfall. Learn more in the Fall River chapter (p.219).

Driving in Rocky

With elevations ranging from 8,000 to over 12,000 feet above sea level, driving in Rocky presents several unique challenges. Steep roads, bad weather, and abundant wildlife all pose dangers not common in the suburbs.

Be prepared for bad weather, including hail and snow, any time of year. This is particularly true at high elevations. Afternoon thunderstorms are common in summer (p.42). Your vehicle, which is insulated from the ground by rubber tires, is one of the safest places to take shelter during a lightning storm.

Steep roads also pose challenges. Trail Ridge Road rises 4,000 feet and has grades of up to 7 percent, which doesn't sound like much but can really wear down your brakes. When driving downhill, use lower gears to reduce reliance on brakes. If you can smell your brakes, you're over-using them.

Reduced oxygen at higher elevations mean engines can lose up to 20 percent of their normal power. Before driving in the park, make sure your vehicle has plenty of gas. When driving uphill, turn off your air conditioner so your engine has more power. Modern fuel-injected engines generally handle elevation well, but older carbureted engines sometimes experience vapor lock. This happens when liquid fuel turns to vapor, making it difficult for pumps to deliver fuel to the engine. Vapor lock can result in power loss, stalling, or vehicles not starting. To fix vapor lock, park your vehicle, loosen the gas cap, open the hood, and wait up to 30 minutes for the fuel system to cool down.

Another driving concern is wildlife. It's not unusual for deer or elk to wander along roads, so always be alert. More dangerous than wildlife are overexcited human drivers, who often brake suddenly when they spot wildlife. Sharpen your defensive driving skills, particularly in autumn, when the elk rut lures thousands of wildlife watchers to the park.

Park Shuttles

Rocky Mountain National Park offers free shuttles between Estes Park, Bear Lake Road, and Moraine Park. Shuttles are excellent alternatives to driving. Instead of fighting traffic and searching for limited parking, you can ride the shuttle, enjoy the views, help the environment, and spend more time outside.

There are three shuttle routes in the park, all of which converge at Park & Ride across from Glacier Basin Campground on Bear Lake Road. Shuttles generally run from late May to mid-October. The purple Hiker Express Route travels between Estes Park Visitor Center and Park & Ride between 7:30am and 8pm. The orange Bear Lake Route travels between Park & Ride and Bear Lake, stopping at Bierstadt Lake Trailhead and Glacier Gorge Trailhead. The green Moraine Park Route travels between Park & Ride and Moraine Park, making half a dozen stops along the way. Shuttle schedules are listed online and in park newspapers.

Parking

All visitors must park in designated parking spaces. Parking on vegetation or other non-designated spaces will result in a ticket.

Gas Stations

There are no gas stations in Rocky Mountain National Park. Gas stations are located just outside the park in the small towns of Estes Park and Grand Lake, but prices are often slightly higher than average. If you're driving to Estes Park, fill up your tank in the town of Lyons. If you're driving to Grand Lake, fill up your tank in the town of Granby.

Biking

Bikes are allowed on all park roads when they are open to vehicles, but bikes are not allowed on any trails. Cyclists must stay to the right, ride single file, and obey all traffic laws. Trail Ridge Road and Old Fall River Road are open to cyclists April 1 to November 30 (except during road maintenance and emergency closures). Cyclists on Old Fall River Road must follow traffic one-way uphill.

Activities

Ranger Programs

Free ranger-led programs are offered year-round, and they are one of the best ways to learn about Rocky Mountain National Park. Topics may include wildlife, birding, geology, history, astronomy, photography, and more. There are also guided hikes, winter snowshoe walks, and evening programs at outdoor amphitheaters. Current ranger-led programs are published in seasonal newspapers, posted at visitor centers, and listed on the park's website.

Junior Rangers

Kids of all ages can complete activity books, earn badges, and become certified Junior Rangers in Rocky Mountain National Park. Free activity books are available at visitor centers, and the park's Junior Ranger headquarters is located at Hidden Valley (p.239) in summer. From late June to mid-August, the Junior Ranger headquarters offers daily programs between 10am and 2:30pm.

Guided Tours

ROCKY MOUNTAIN CONSERVANCY

The nonprofit partner of Rocky Mountain National Park (p.38) offers a wide variety of excellent hands-on learning experiences. Options include Trail Ridge Road bus tours, hiking trips, and classes specializing in geology, birdwatching, photography, outdoor skills, wildflowers, and much more (rmconservancy.org).

COLORADO MOUNTAIN SCHOOL

If you're interested in challenging outdoor adventures, contact Colorado Mountain School. Since 1981, CMS has offered classes specializing in rock climbing, mountaineering, ice climbing, backcountry skiing, avalanche training, and more. (coloradomountainschool.com)

KIRKS MOUNTAIN ADVENTURES

Guided day hikes, overnight backpacks, and llama pack trips where llamas carry up to 80 pounds of gear or children. (kirksmountainadventures.com)

WILD SIDE 4X4 TOURS

Guided tours in customized off-road vehicles. Wild Side offers trips in the park and on rugged roads in adjacent national forests (wildside4x4tours.com).

GREEN JEEP TOURS

Guided Jeep tours on Trail Ridge Road, Fall River Road, and other popular roads in the park. Tours are also available outside the park (greenjeeptour.com).

Hazards & Safety

Wildlife

Rocky is famous for abundant wildlife, but you should *always* keep a safe distance while viewing wild animals. Try to stay at least 75 feet (two bus lengths) away from elk and bighorn sheep. Stay at least 120 feet away from moose and bears. Note to photographers: A good telephoto lens is cheaper than a hospital bill.

During the elk rut in September and October, foot traffic is not allowed from 5pm to 10am around Moraine Park, Upper Beaver Meadows, Horseshoe Park, Harbison Meadow, and the meadow next to Holzwarth Historic Site.

Mountain lion sightings are *extremely* rare, but if you do encounter a lion, give it *plenty* of space. If a mountain lion approaches, pick up children and back away slowly. If a mountain lion becomes aggressive, shout, wave your arms, and throw objects at it. Try to signal that you are a potential predator, not prey. If the mountain lion attacks, fight back.

Altitude Sickness

Rocky has the highest average elevation of any national park in America, with elevations ranging from 8,000 to 14,259 feet above sea level. Some visitors experience altitude sickness due to low oxygen levels. If you're visiting from sea level, rangers recommend spending at least one night at 7,000–8,000 feet (Estes Park sits at 7,500 feet, Grand Lake sits at 8,400 feet) before venturing into higher parts of the park. Be sure to drink plenty of liquids. Symptoms of altitude sickness include headache, nausea, fatigue, dizziness, and vomiting. The only cure is quickly descending to lower elevations.

Lightning

There are nearly half a million lightning strikes in Colorado each year, including hundreds in Rocky Mountain National Park. Thunderstorms are most common in the afternoon during monsoon season (July, August), but lightning strikes can happen year-round. Exposed, high-elevation areas are the most dangerous places to be. Always scan the horizon for approaching thunderstorms. If you can hear thunder, seek shelter or descend to lower elevations. Buildings and vehicles are the safest places to be. If you can't make it to a building or vehicle, seek shelter away from summits, ridgetops, and stand-alone trees. In forested areas, crouch near shrubs or bushes. Always avoid bodies of water.

Ticks

Tick bites can transmit diseases to humans, and the best prevention is reducing exposed skin. After spending time outdoors, check your body for ticks, which like to crawl into hard-to-reach places, like armpits and groin. If you find a tick, remove it with tweezers and be sure to remove the pinchers. Place the tick in a ziplock bag for analysis if you develop symptoms later. Many tick bites are harmless, and infected ticks must attach for up to day to transmit disease.

Colorado Tick Fever is a tick-borne virus with symptoms similar to flu: fever, chills, headache, nausea, vomiting. Symptoms occur four to five days after a tick bite. The disease is generally mild, and the only cure is bed rest.

Rocky Mountain Spotted Fever is a tick-borne microorganism that causes flu-like symptoms and a rash that starts on the hands and feet. The rash then spreads to the rest of the body. Symptoms occur about 10 days after a tick bite. It is easily treated with antibiotics. Despite the name, there are very few cases in Colorado.

Giardiasis

This gastrointestinal disease is caused by microorganisms in water. Avoid drinking untreated water from rivers, streams, lakes, and ponds. Symptoms (abdominal pain, cramps, diarrhea) occur seven to 10 days after drinking infected water.

Rocky Mountain Conservancy

This wonderful nonprofit, founded in 1931, promotes stewardship of Rocky Mountain National Park through education and philanthropy. It funds park projects, operates interpretive stores in visitor centers, offers hands-on learning experiences through their Field Institute, and organizes youth Conservation Corps. Membership benefits include a 15 percent discount at stores, discounts on Field Institute programs, a subscription to a quarterly newsletter, and invitations to special events. Learn more at rmconservancy.org.

Lodging

There's no lodging in the park, but there are plenty of hotels in gateway towns just outside the park. Visit jameskaiser.com for lodging recommendations.

Camping in Rocky

The park has five campgrounds (three reserveable, two first-come, first-served). Visit recreation.gov for campground reservations.

GLACIER BASIN CAMPGROUND

Located along Bear Lake Road, across from Park & Ride. 150 campsites. $30 per night. Reservations required. Open late May to mid-September.

MORAINE PARK CAMPGROUND

Located just north of Moraine Park. 244 campsites. Reservations required. $30 per night. Open year-round. First-come, first-served in winter.

ASPENGLEN CAMPGROUND

Located near Fall River Entrance along Fall River. 52 campsites. $30 per night. Open late May to mid-September. Reservations required.

LONGS PEAK CAMPGROUND

Located next to Longs Peak Trailhead. 26 campsites. $30 per night. Open late June to early September. First-come, first-served.

TIMBER CREEK CAMPGROUND

The only campground on the west side of the park. 98 campsites. $30 per night. Open late May to late September. First-come, first-served.

Camping outside Rocky

There are over a dozen public and private campgrounds outside the park, ranging from luxurious (hot showers, swimming pools) to spartan (primitive camping in national forests). Visit jameskaiser.com for a complete list of recommended camping options outside the park.

One Perfect Day in Rocky

Most visitors starting from Estes Park head straight to Bear Lake (p.149), which boasts some of the best hiking trails in the park. But Bear Lake is generally crowded in the morning, particularly during peak season. Rather than battle morning crowds, drive up Trail Ridge Road (p.237) or Old Fall River Road (p.219). You'll enjoy some of the most spectacular views in the park bathed in beautiful morning light. After crossing the Continental Divide, spend the late morning exploring Kawuneeche Valley (p.273), where there are plenty of great hikes. Enjoy a picnic lunch on the trail or visit one of the restaurants just outside the park in Grand Lake (p.52). Return via Trail Ridge Road in mid-afternoon, then visit Bear Lake in late afternoon, when there are fewer crowds. On the way back, stop at beautiful Moraine Park (p.133). Depending on the time of day, you might enjoy a fabulous sunset framed by Moraine Park's dramatic Front Range peaks. Consider checking out an evening ranger program at Moraine Park Campground Amphitheater (p.140), then head back to Estes Park for dinner (p.48). Before going to bed, don't forget to look up at the stars (p.30). Note: if you drive across the park to Kawuneeche Valley between July and September, consider driving up Fall River Road, then returning via Trail Ridge Road. Combining the two roads makes a dramatic loop with plenty of bold alpine scenery.

Another Perfect Day in Rocky

After exploring the park's famous highlights (Bear Lake, Trail Ridge Road, Kawuneeche Valley), head to the rugged southern end of Rocky Mountain National Park, where Longs Peak, the tallest mountain in the park (p.196), towers over the rugged scenery. Creature comforts are minimal, but Longs Peak and Wild Basin (p.177) are home to lots of great hiking trails. From easy waterfall strolls to challenging hikes to alpine lakes, there's a trail for everyone here. Enjoy a picnic lunch in the park, or head back to Estes Park. When you return, be sure to check out some of the interesting sights on Highway 7 (p.179), including beautiful Lily Lake (p.180), where an easy trail loops around the shore. In late afternoon you can stroll around Lake Estes (p.50). Or, if you're up for more hiking, head to Lumpy Ridge (p.211). Towering above the north end of Estes Park, Lumpy Ridge has two great hikes that begin just a short drive from downtown: an easy hike to the base of Twin Owls (p.214) and a more challenging hike to beautiful Gem Lake (p.216). Finish the day with dinner in Estes Park, followed by a movie at one of the oldest movie theaters in America (p.51). After the movie ends, take a moonlight stroll along the Estes Park Riverwalk (p.50).

When to Visit

SPRING

Conditions in spring are highly variable, fluctuating between warm, cold, wet, and dry. Much depends on winter snowfall, which can keep roads closed and trails icy/muddy into late spring. Elevation also plays a significant role. By late April, spring often arrives at lower elevations (8,000–9,500 feet), bringing warmer temperatures and beautiful wildflowers. By early June, spring often migrates to subalpine country (9,500 to 11,500 feet). Trail Ridge Road normally opens in late May, but following the snowiest winters it can stay closed until June.

SUMMER

Summer is the park's most popular season. You can drive or hike to the park's highest elevations, enjoying balmy temperatures during the day. But summer also brings big crowds and thunderstorms. During monsoon season (July, August), afternoon thunderstorms roll through the mountains nearly every day. Blue skies can fill with dark clouds in under an hour—always pack rain gear. Wildflowers bloom in alpine tundra from late June to early August. The park's highest elevations experience a season most accurately called "non-winter" from early June to mid-September. Conditions can change rapidly. At Alpine Visitor Center, located on Trail Ridge Road 11,796 feet above sea level, it can snow any day of the year.

AUTUMN

Autumn is my favorite season in the park. The weather is glorious: warm, sunny days in early September turning to crisp, sunny days by early October. In mid-September, golden aspen light up the mountains, with foliage generally peaking in early October. September is also the start of the annual elk rut, when the haunting bugle of dominant bulls echoes through the park. Not surprisingly, September is one of the park's most popular months. In terms of total visitation, September is comparable to July and August, but visitation is 50 percent higher on September weekends. By mid-October, leaves, temperatures, and visitation numbers all drop in unison. By late October, Trail Ridge Road usually closes for the season.

WINTER

Temperatures and visitation numbers plummet in winter—which is why some people *love* visiting park during this time. In addition to breathtaking snow-capped mountains, there's great snowshoeing and cross-country skiing. Sledding is only allowed at Hidden Valley. Hardcore adventure junkies enjoy backcountry skiing, winter mountaineering, and ice climbing. There's often snow on the ground by December, but January, February, and March are generally the snowiest months. Avalanches are common in winter, and avalanche training is recommended for anyone spending time in the backcountry. Note: Although overall winter visitation is relatively low, weekends and holidays can be busy.

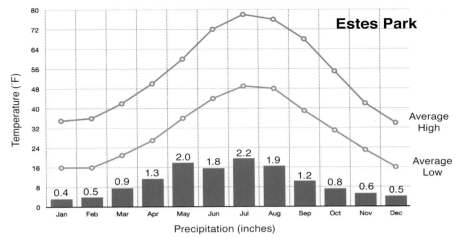

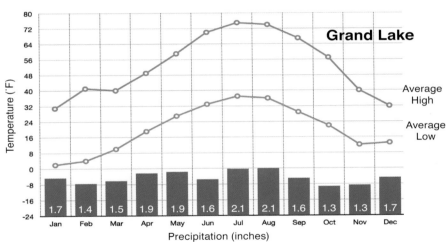

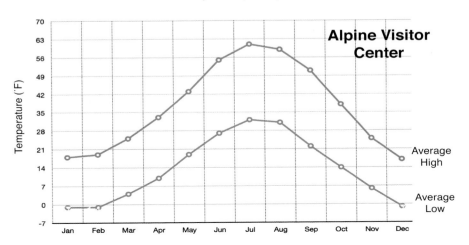

Rocky Mountain Weather

Colorado boasts over 300 days of sunshine per year, but weather in the mountains can be highly unpredictable. Sunburns and snowstorms are both possible in July. To plan a successful visit to Rocky Mountain National Park, you should know a few basics about local weather patterns.

Colorado's weather is influenced by two major factors: its location in the continental interior and its rugged topography among the Rockies' highest peaks. Because Colorado is situated hundreds of miles from the Pacific Ocean and the Gulf of Mexico, wind that blows over the state is relatively dry. Prevailing winds arrive from the west and blow up and over the mountains. As a general rule, temperatures decrease about 3–4° F for every 1,000 feet of elevation gain. When air blows up the Rockies' western slope it cools and condenses, releasing precipitation in the form of rain or snow. Robbed of its scant moisture, dry air blows across the eastern plains. From April through early September, however, moist air from the Gulf of Mexico sometimes blows north, bringing heavy precipitation to the plains and the eastern slope of the Rockies.

Summer thunderstorms are common in Rocky Mountain National Park. Tall mountains absorb the sun's heat faster than lower elevations, generating thermals that rise into the atmosphere. As warm air rises it cools and condenses, forming enormous thunderclouds called cumulonimbus clouds. By afternoon these dark clouds can tower 30,000 feet above sea level. When the top of a cumulonimbus cloud reaches the stratosphere, it flattens out, forming an anvil shape that can stretch hundreds of miles across. These enormous clouds, which contain the energy of several atomic bombs, release their moisture in powerful thunderstorms. In summer, the Rockies are essentially a giant thunderstorm factory. Prevailing winds generally push storms east over the plains, leaving clear skies in the mountains at night. Thunderstorms are common from June through early September. Always be prepared for rain, and understand the dangers of lightning (p.37), particularly when exploring the park's highest elevations.

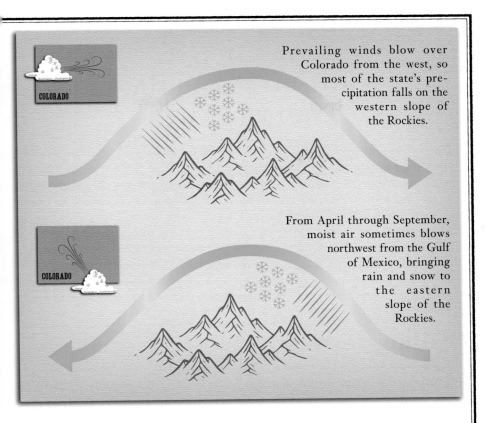

Prevailing winds blow over Colorado from the west, so most of the state's precipitation falls on the western slope of the Rockies.

From April through September, moist air sometimes blows northwest from the Gulf of Mexico, bringing rain and snow to the eastern slope of the Rockies.

Winter brings powerful winds to the Front Range of the Rockies. The strongest winds occur above treeline (11,000 to 11,500 feet), where wind speeds average about 50 mph but often blow 100 mph or more. Occasionally the jet stream dips down and touches Longs Peak, bringing gusts that can top 200 mph! Another winter phenomenon is Chinook winds, which roar down the eastern slope and deliver gusts that can exceed 100 mph in Boulder and Fort Collins. As Chinook winds race down from high elevations, the air quickly compresses, causing it to warm and dry out. Chinook winds are sometimes called "snow killers" because they melt snow so quickly. Similar to Chinook winds are Bora winds, which also flow down from the mountains but deliver blasts of cold air after the passage of a strong cold front. Bora winds are most common in spring and fall.

Valley winds are another weather phenomenon influenced by local topography. On sunny days warm air flows up mountain valleys, resulting in warm afternoon breezes. At night cold air from high peaks flows down mountain valleys, resulting in cool early morning breezes. Valley winds are most common during calm and clear weather.

Death in Rocky Mountain National Park

Rocky's beautiful landscape lures millions of visitors each year, but the park's rugged mountains should never be taken for granted. Falls, freezing temperatures, and freak accidents have claimed over 300 lives since the park was established in 1915. Each year, the park conducts dozens of search-and-rescue operations. As with any natural area, Rocky Mountain National Park comes with inherent risks. The majority of deaths in the park involve males (particularly young males) but accidents can happen to visitors of any age or gender. Be aware of the park's unique hazards (p.36), and always exercise caution. When in doubt, seek advice from a park ranger. Also remember that the average number of annual deaths in recent years (four to five) is small compared to the total number of annual visitors (four to five million).

Falling Deaths

Deadly falls have claimed over 100 lives in Rocky Mountain National Park. Nearly half of those falls occurred on Longs Peak. Other potentially deadly mountains include Mount Meeker, Mount MacGregor, Ypsilon Mountain, Twin Sisters, Deer Mountain, and Little Matterhorn. Deadly or life-threatening falls have also occurred at popular viewpoints. These falls often involve visitors venturing beyond guardrails, engaging in risky behavior, or getting too close to a dropoff while posing for a dramatic photo.

Longs Peak

Over 70 people have perished on the tallest mountain in the park. Falls account for over half of all deaths on Longs Peak, while hypothermia is the second biggest killer. Three people have died from lightning strikes. Perhaps the most bizarre death involved a young man who climbed Longs Peak in 1889 with a pistol that accidentally fired, leaving him with a mortal wound.

Motor Vehicles

Roughly 30 visitors have died in motor vehicle accidents, making driving one of the deadliest activities in the park. Rocky's high mountain roads and many distractions (majestic wildlife, beautiful views) add an extra element of danger. Always follow speed limits, and use extra caution while driving in the park.

Hypothermia

Over one dozen people have died of hypothermia in Rocky Mountain National Park. Most hypothermia deaths occur on Longs Peak, but freezing temperatures have claimed lives in far gentler areas. Many deaths occur after the weather suddenly changes, which is common in the Rockies. Freezing temperatures and hypothermia are possible any time of year, including summer. When exploring the mountains, always bring warm clothes. Symptoms of hypothermia include sleepiness, impaired judgment, shivering, and slurred speech.

Lightning Strikes

Over one dozen people have died from lightning strikes in the park. Trail Ridge Road and Longs Peak have experienced the most fatal lightning strikes. Lightning can happen year-round, but it is most common in summer.

Drowning

Nearly twenty people have drowned in rivers and streams that flow through the park. Roughly half of those drowning deaths were children under the age of 15. Big Thompson River and North St. Vrain Creek are the two deadliest rivers in the park. Chasm Falls and Adams Falls have also claimed lives. Rivers and streams are most dangerous in spring and summer, when rapidly melting snow generates high waters. Stay out of rivers and streams, and avoid stepping on wet, slippery rocks nearby.

Avalanches

Colorado has the most avalanche deaths of any state, averaging roughly six deaths per year. In Rocky Mountain National Park, avalanches have killed six people. Skiers and mountain climbers are at highest risk.

Wildlife

The park's only recorded wildlife fatality occurred in 1997, when a mountain lion attacked a 10-year-old boy. The child wandered in front of his parents while hiking on the North Inlet Trail. An autopsy revealed the boy died choking on his own vomit during the attack.

Winter Sports

Skiing has claimed two lives in the park. Sledding and snow tubing accidents have killed three people. Today sledding and snow tubing are only allowed at Hidden Valley.

Estes Park

GATEWAY TOWNS

ESTES PARK

Estes Park (pronounced "Estiss" by locals) lies just east of Rocky Mountain National Park's two most popular entrances. The physical setting—a lush mountain valley perched 7,600 feet above sea level, surrounded by towering peaks—is worthy of its own national park, and Estes Park's historic downtown is filled with shops and restaurants. The town is home to roughly 6,500 year-round residents, but it feels much larger in summer, when millions of visitors pass through. Because there's no lodging in Rocky Mountain National Park, most visitors spend the night in Estes Park. From rustic campgrounds to luxury hotels, there's no shortage of options. Visit jameskaiser.com for a complete list of camping and lodging recommendations in Estes Park.

ESTES PARK VISITOR CENTER

Located at intersection of U.S. highways 34 and 36, this is a great first stop within walking distance of both downtown Estes Park and Lake Estes. Adjacent to the visitor center is a large parking garage. This is also the main transport hub for the town's free shuttles.

ESTES PARK SHUTTLES

During peak season, free shuttles operate in both Estes Park and Rocky Mountain National Park. The Estes Park shuttle has five routes that cover most of the town (estespark.colorado.gov/shuttles). The Hiker's Express Route travels between Estes Park Visitor Center and Park & Ride (p.151), a transport hub in Rocky Mountain National Park where you can catch additional shuttles (nps.gov/romo).

Groceries

Safeway (451 East Wonderview Ave.) is the largest grocery store in Estes Park. The Country Market (900 Moraine Ave.), located near Beaver Meadows Entrance, also has a good selection.

Estes Park Restaurants

★ SEASONED AMERICAN BISTRO $$$ (Din)

Exquisite dishes and elegant wines, served in a charming restaurant overlooking Bond Park. Seasonally creative cuisine with local ingredients and global influences, from duck schnitzel to carne asada. 970-586-9000, 205 Park Ln.

★ ROCK INN MOUNTAIN TAVERN $$$ (Lnch, Din)

Delicious Western fare in a relaxed, rustic atmosphere. Juicy steaks, elk sausage, bison meatballs, trout, salmon, salads, and sandwiches. No reservations, try to arrive before 6pm during peak season. 970-586-4116, 1675 State Highway 66.

★ SCRATCH DELI & BAKERY $$$ (Brk, Lnch)

The best picnic outfitter in Estes Park. Homemade bread, delicious sandwiches, fresh pastries, breakfast burritos, great coffee. Located near the park's Beaver Meadows Entrance. 970-586-8383, 911 Moraine Ave.

★ NEPAL'S CAFE $$$ (Lnch, Din)

What better place to enjoy authentic Himalayan cuisine than a high-elevation mountain town? Nepal's offers a savory mix of Nepalese, Tibetan, and Indian classics. 970-577-7035, 184 East Elkhorn Ave.

WHISKEY BAR $$$ (Lnch, Din)

Located in the Stanley Hotel, this elegant lounge boasts Colorado's largest collection of whiskeys and single malt scotches. The menu includes tasty burgers, pastas, steaks, and elk/bison meatloaf. 970-577-4000, 333 Wonderview Ave.

SMOKIN' DAVE'S BBQ $$$ (Lnch, Din)

Texas beef brisket, Carolina pulled pork, St. Louis pork ribs, cheddar jalapeño sausage—indulge your carnivorous habits. Classic Southern side dishes and great beers on tap. 970-577-7427, 820 Moraine Ave.

NOTCHTOP CAFE $$$ (Brk, Lnch)

Big breakfasts (benedicts, hashes, pancakes, waffles, burritos) and tasty lunches (sandwiches, wraps, pitas, burgers, pitas, salads). Plenty of vegan, vegetarian, and gluten-free options. 970-586-0272, 459 East Wonderview Ave.

LA COCINA DE MAMA $$$ (Brk, Lnch, Din)

Tasty Mexican classics: tacos, burritos, enchiladas, quesadillas, tamales, chimichangas, menudo, pozole. 970-586-9001, 361 S. Saint Vrain Ave.

OPPA ASIAN BISTRO $$$ (Lnch, Din)

Korean favorites (bulgogi, bibimbap, kimchi fried rice) and Asian flavors (curry, tempura, udon noodles). 970-577-8888, 183 West Riverside Drive.

The Stanley Hotel

For over a century, the Stanley Hotel has been the most elegant and dramatic hotel in Estes Park. Perched on a hill overlooking Lake Estes, it was built by F.O. Stanley, the multimillionaire inventor of dry plate photography and the Stanley Steamer automobile. Inspired by classic East Coast architecture (Stanley was originally from Maine), the hotel featured modern luxuries including electric lights and telephones when it opened in 1909. F.O. Stanley entertained guests in lavish style. The concert hall still has a trap door built for a performance by Harry Houdini. By the 1970s, however, the once-grand hotel had fallen into disrepair. Then, in 1974, a young writer named Stephen King spent one night at The Stanley. The nearly vacant hotel was about to shut down for winter, and King spent the night drinking at the bar. King's stay inspired him to write *The Shining*, his third major novel and first hardcover bestseller. The blockbuster film, directed by Stanley Kubrick, spurred the hotel's revival, but The Stanley never appeared in the film. Exterior scenes were filmed at Timberline Lodge at Mount Hood, Oregon, and interior sets were based on the Ahwahnee Hotel in Yosemite National Park. King was so unhappy with Kubrick's version that he wanted to shoot a remake at The Stanley. That film was never made, but King did supervise a 1997 TV version of *The Shining* shot at the hotel. The Stanley also served as the fictional Hotel Danbury in the comedy *Dumb and Dumber*. Tours of The Stanley, including a haunted night tour, are available to the public year-round (stanleyhotel.com).

Estes Park Notable

★ LAKE ESTES

Nestled in the heart of Estes Park, this 185-acre lake is one of the best places to soak in the town's spectacular scenery. Two paved paths parallel the northern and southern shores, leading to picnic tables, beaches, and viewpoints. Lake Estes Marina, located on the northeast shore, rents bikes, pedal carts, kayaks, canoes, SUPs, and motor boats. (1770 Big Thompson Ave, 970-586-2011)

★ DOWNTOWN RIVERWALK

A beautiful one-mile riverwalk stretches from Estes Park Visitor Center to Performance Park Amphitheater. Perched above Big Thompson River and Fall River, it feels a world away from the cars and crowds on East Elkhorn Avenue, yet still offers easy access to great shops and restaurants.

★ MACDONALD BOOK SHOP

This independent bookstore has hundreds of thoughtfully curated titles, including an impressive selection of books about Rocky Mountain National Park and Colorado. (152 East Elkhorn, macdonaldbookshop.com)

ESTES PARK AERIAL TRAMWAY

Ride to the top of 8,900-foot Prospect Mountain on this aerial tram, in operation since 1955. At the top there's an observation platform and coffee shop, plus hiking trails around the summit. (420 East Riverside Drive, estestram.com)

THE PARK THEATER

Built in 1913, the Park Theater is the oldest continually operating movie theater in the U.S. The lobby is filled with historic movie paraphernalia, and the theatre shows a mix of new and classic films. (130 Moraine Ave., historicparktheatre.com)

ESTES PARK MUSEUM

Estes Park has a wild and colorful history, and it's all on display at this charming museum, including a Stanley Steamer automobile. The museum bookstore has lots of great local titles. (200 4th St., estes.org/museum)

YMCA OF THE ROCKIES

Located on the eastern boundary of Rocky Mountain National Park, this YMCA is so big it has its own ZIP code. There's overnight lodging, and activities range from hiking to astronomy to sledding to axe-throwing. (ymcarockies.org)

ROOFTOP RODEO

This classic "Rodeo with Altitude!" is considered one of the best in Colorado. It features bull riding, barrel-racing, team roping, and rodeo clowns. The Rooftop Rodeo is held each year in early July. (rooftoprodeo.com)

SCOTTISH-IRISH HIGHLAND FESTIVAL

One of the largest Scottish-Irish festivals in America attracts thousands of kilt-wearing, bagpipe-blasting revelers. Held the first weekend after Labor Day. It kicks off with a huge parade in downtown Estes Park. (scotfest.com)

GRAND LAKE

Located just outside the park's western entrance, Grand Lake is the largest and deepest natural lake in Colorado. Situated 8,400 feet above sea level, it reflects the park's majestic peaks, and the adjacent town (population 500) revolves around national park tourism and lakeside fun. Two larger man-made reservoirs, Shadow Mountain Lake and Lake Granby, lie just south of Grand Lake. In 2020, the explosive East Troublesome Fire nearly destroyed the town of Grand Lake, which survived thanks to the heroic efforts of firefighters (p.130). It will take time for the surrounding forests to recover, but the tiny town and pristine lake remain as charming as ever.

Grand Lake has a surface area of 507 acres and a maximum depth of 389 feet. It formed after the Ice Age, when the terminal moraine of a retreating glacier created a natural dam. Nearby Shadow Mountain Lake (1,346 acres) and Lake Granby (7,250 acres) are man-made reservoirs created in the 1940s and '50s as part of the Big Thompson Water Project. Water from Lake Granby is pumped 125 vertical feet into Shadow Mountain Lake, which flows into Grand Lake. Water then flows through the 17-mile Alva B. Adams Tunnel under Rocky Mountain National Park and the Continental Divide to the Big Thompson River. It is Colorado's largest west-east water project, pumping 300,000 acre-feet of water each year. This additional water helps sustain the thirsty East Slope, where 80% of Colorado's population resides.

Grand Lake Restaurants

★ RAPIDS LODGE $$$ (Din)
Perched above a beautiful stretch of North Inlet River, the restaurant at Rapids Lodge has an excellent selection of Colorado meats (steak, lamb, elk medallions), plus burgers, salmon, and pasta. Good wines. 970-627-3707, 210 Rapids Ln.

★ BACKSTREET STEAKHOUSE $$$ (Din)
This cozy restaurant (part of Daven Haven Lodge) offers a nice selection of steaks, tasty burgers, seafood, and pasta, plus salads and vegetarian options. The outdoor patio has live music in summer. 970-627-8144, 604 Marina Drive.

★ HUNTINGTON HOUSE TAVERN $$$
Located at Grand Lake Lodge, Hunting House Tavern combines rustic classics (steak, venison, trout, striped bass) with spectacular views high above Grand Lake. Sandwiches, soups, and salads for lunch. 970-627-3967, 15500 U.S. 34.

GRAND PIZZA $$$ (Lnch, Din)
Serves—you guessed it—delicious pizza with a long list of toppings. Calzones, pasta, and salads round out the menu. 970-627-8390, 1131 Grand Ave.

Grand Lake Notable

★ GRAND LAKE BOARDWALK
Set two blocks back from Grand Lake on Grand Ave, this quaint wooden boardwalk is lined with shops and restaurants. Start at Ellsworth Street, end at Hancock Street, then head south to Town Beach on the north shore of Grand Lake.

★ WATER SPORTS
Getting out on the water is one of the highlights of Grand Lake. Grand Lake Marina (glmarina.com) rents motorboats, SUPs, kayaks, and canoes. Trail Ridge Marina (trailridgemarina.com) offers a similar selection of rentals on Shadow Mountain Reservoir.

★ ROCKY MOUNTAIN REPERTORY THEATRE
This local gem, which draws talented actors and musicians from around the country, stages impressive Broadway musicals in season. Tickets are available at the box office, over the phone, or online (970-627-3421, rockymountainrep.com).

NEVER SUMMER MOUNTAIN PRODUCTS
The place to go for outdoor gear in Grand Lake. Kayak and SUP rentals in summer, cross-country ski and snowshoe rentals in winter. 970-627-3642, 919 Grand Ave.

Legends of Grand Lake

For centuries Grand Lake was a gathering place for local tribes. Both the Utes and Arapahoes visited the large lake, but long ago a confrontation erupted between the two tribes. The Utes put their women and children on a raft, which they sent to the center of the lake for safety. While the tribes fought, a powerful windstorm whipped up the waters. The raft capsized, drowning all aboard, and from that day forward the Utes avoided the lake, which was haunted by the spirits of the dead.

The Arapaho tell the story of mysterious bison tracks discovered on top of the frozen lake. The unusually large tracks emerged from a hole in the center of the lake, indicating that a supernatural bison lived in the waters. For this reason the Arapahoes call the lake *batan-náach*, "Spirit Lake."

GEOLOGY

ROCKY MOUNTAIN NATIONAL PARK is a high-altitude wonderland showcasing some of the finest alpine geology in America. From 8,000-foot-high meadows to the top of 14,259-foot Longs Peak, the park's lofty terrain tells a remarkable story nearly two billion years in the making. It involves colliding continents, erupting volcanoes, enormous Ice Age glaciers, and countless other splendid catastrophes.

Most visitors are happy to simply visit and enjoy the views. But take some time to learn about the forces that created the landscape and you'll look upon the park with a fresh set of eyes. What was once amazing will become astounding. What once took your breath away will make your head spin.

The park's oldest rocks formed roughly two billion years ago—nearly half the age of earth and comparable to the oldest rocks at the bottom of Grand Canyon. At the time Colorado was mostly covered by ocean, with a few scattered islands poking above the water. Over millions of years, eroded sediments compressed into sedimentary rocks. Sandy beaches became sandstone and thick layers of mud became shale. Back then life was in its infancy. Single-cell organisms floated in the oceans, but continents were barren and lifeless, more similar to Mars than the landscapes we know today.

Roughly 1.7 billion years ago, the sedimentary rocks were caught in a collision of continents. As tectonic plates smashed into each other, they thrust up an ancient mountain range—a geologic event called the Colorado Orogeny. (*Orogeny* comes from the Greek words *oros*, "mountain," and *genesis*, "creation.") Exposed to extreme heat and pressure, the previously formed sandstone and shale metamorphosed into the metamorphic rocks gneiss and schist.

The next 300 million years were relatively quiet. Erosion slowly ground down the mountains, tectonic plates continued to shift, and cracks formed in the metamorphic rocks. Then, roughly 1.4 billion years ago, an enormous plume of magma rose under present-day Rocky Mountain National Park. Tendrils of magma seeped into cracks in the overlying metamorphic rocks, and when they cooled they formed veins of granite. When the larger magma plume cooled below, it formed a 600-square-mile mass of granite, called a batholith, deep underground. These metamorphic and granite rocks, which formed during the Proterozoic Eon (2.5 billion years ago to 542 million years ago), would one day make up most of the rocks in Rocky Mountain National Park.

Over the next one billion years, erosion slowly ground down the once-towering mountains. During the Paleozoic Era (542–251 million years ago), shallow seas washed over Colorado, and tens of thousands of feet of sedimentary rocks formed over the Proterozoic rocks. Fish, insects, reptiles, trees, and land plants all evolved during this time.

Ancestral Rocky Mountains

Around 320 million years ago, a new mountain range, the Ancestral Rocky Mountains, started to rise. This event coincided with the earth's continents smashing together to form the supercontinent Pangea. The North American portion of Pangea lay near the equator, Colorado sat near the west coast, and the Ancestral Rockies were mountainous islands rising above a tropical sea.

As erosion chipped away at the Ancestral Rocky Mountains, reddish sediments washed down and formed new sedimentary rocks that would one day become the Flatirons in Boulder, Red Rocks Amphitheater in Denver, and Aspen's Maroon Bells. By the end of the Paleozoic Era, roughly 251 million years ago, erosion had reduced the Ancestral Rocky Mountains to a fraction of their previous size.

The end of the Paleozoic is marked by the largest mass extinction in history. Roughly 90 percent of all species died. It was triggered by massive volcanic eruptions in Siberia, which led to extreme ocean acidification and climate change. The great die-off marked the start of the Mesozoic Era (251–66 million years ago), when surviving reptiles evolved into dinosaurs. Small mammals also appeared during this time, but their evolution was hindered by marauding dinosaurs.

Around 200 million years ago, Pangea split down the middle. Europe and Africa drifted east, and enormous quantities of magma and noxious gases poured forth from the seams. This led to runaway global warming, triggering another mass extinction that killed over 30 percent of all species. In the wake of the die-off, dinosaurs reigned supreme, ushering in the Jurassic period.

By the early Jurassic, erosion had ground down the Ancestral Rockies to mere hills, which were then swallowed by the largest sand dune desert the world has ever known. At their peak, the dunes covered 150,000 square miles, including much of Colorado. Toward the end of the Jurassic, 150 million years ago, sea levels rose and the Arctic Ocean migrated south. Marine waters advanced and retreated over Colorado multiple times, eventually leaving behind a vast lowland of lakes, swamps, and streams. Although deposits from this era are absent in Rocky Mountain National Park, elsewhere in Colorado they have yielded some of the most impressive dinosaur fossils ever discovered.

Around 100 million years ago, the Gulf of Mexico migrated north, creating the Western Interior Seaway, which split North America in two. Most of Colorado was submerged during this time. Aquatic dinosaurs and 30-foot sharks swam in the waters for roughly 30 million years, until the inland sea retreated. By that point, however, a new mountain-building episode had already begun.

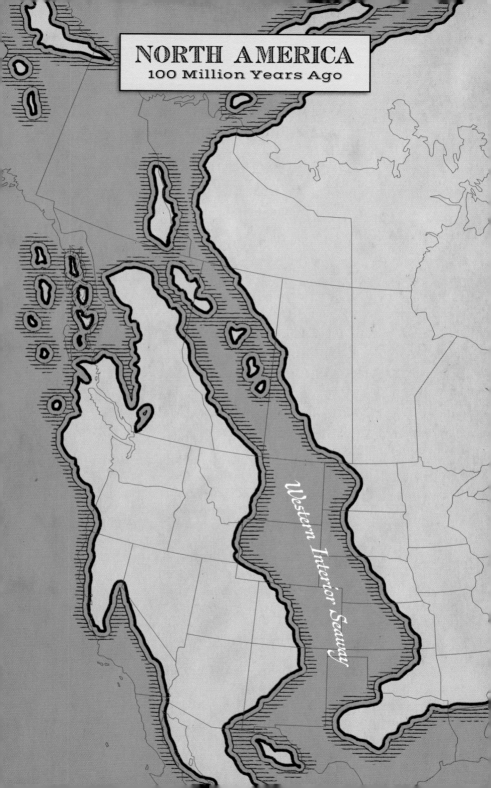

NORTH AMERICA
100 Million Years Ago

Western Interior Seaway

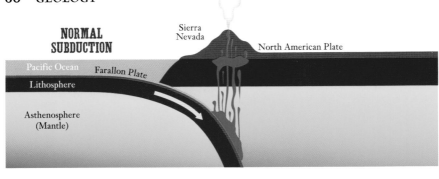

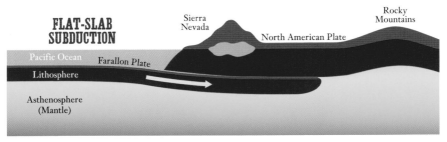

Laramide Orogeny

Near the end of the age of dinosaurs, the modern Rocky Mountains started to rise. This event, called the Laramide Orogeny, was triggered by plate tectonics—specifically the Farallon Plate, which lay off the west coast of North America, colliding with the North American Plate. Starting around 210 million years ago, the North American Plate overrode the Farallon Plate, which pushed the eastern edge of the Farallon Plate deep underground in a process called subduction. As the Farallon Plate subducted, it came into contact with earth's hot mantle. Giant plumes of magma rose under California, creating the Sierra Nevada Mountains.

Then, roughly 80 million years ago, magma stopped rising under California. Around the same time, 600 miles east, the modern Rocky Mountains started to rise. Geologists suspect the two events are related, but the exact mechanisms remain hotly debated. One theory says the Farallon Plate's angle of subduction changed around 80 million years ago, initiating a period of flat-slab subduction that shifted the mountain-building process to the interior of the continent.

As the Rockies rose, the Western Interior Seaway drained, leaving Colorado high and dry. The continental crust broke into blocks, some of which uplifted to become mountains, while others fell to become basins. Over millions of years, erosion removed the overlying sedimentary rocks, exposing the schist, gneiss, and granite that had formed over one billion years earlier.

Around 67 million years ago, Colorado had a warm, rainy climate, and Tyrannosaurus rex prowled the land. Then, without warning, an asteroid the size of Denver struck the Yucatan Peninsula with the force of 10 billion atomic bombs.

Over 1,000 miles away in Colorado, powerful earthquakes shook the ground, scalding hot debris rained down from the sky, and forests spontaneously ignited. In the aftermath of the asteroid blast, dinosaurs went extinct, setting the stage for the rise of the mammals.

Over the next 25 million years, as small rodents evolved into much larger creatures, the Rocky Mountains continued their rise. During this time, hot, mineral-rich fluids percolated through the mountains, depositing gold and silver and forming the Colorado Mineral Belt. The rise of the Rockies was a constant battle between uplift and erosion, however, and by about 37 million years ago, many of the peaks were buried in their own debris. Broad, undulating highlands characterized much of the landscape.

As tectonic plates shifted, volcanic activity broke out across much of Colorado, possibly due to the final subduction of the Farallon Plate under the west coast of North America. Deep faults formed on the west side of present-day Rocky Mountain National Park, stretching the land and bringing magma to the surface. Between 29 and 24 million years ago, erupting volcanoes spewed lava across the landscape, forming the ancient ancestors of today's Never Summer Mountains.

The same forces that triggered volcanic activity may have also warmed the mantle under Colorado, forming a giant blister that pushed up the Rockies again. Erosion eventually buried the mountains in their own debris, and by about 10 million years ago the Rockies were largely an elevated extension of the Great Plains. Then, over the past five million years, erosion flushed out the debris that buried the Rockies and covered the Great Plains. This may have been partly due to global cooling that increased precipitation and accelerated erosion. Rivers and streams tumbled down the gently rounded mountains, carving steep V-shaped valleys into their sides. The broad contours of the modern mountains had finally taken shape. But it would take one last dramatic act of geology to put the finishing touches on the Rockies.

The Ice Age

Around 2.5 million years ago, earth entered the Ice Age. Scientists are unsure what triggered this period of global cooling, but one culprit is earth's wobbly orbit. When earth wobbles one way, solar radiation decreases and temperatures drop. When earth wobbles the other way, solar radiation increases and temperatures rise. These natural cycles, called Milankovitch cycles, generally last about 100,000 years. Cold periods last about 80,000–90,000 years, and warm periods in between last about 10,000–20,000 years.

As global temperatures dropped, thick layers of snow accumulated in the Arctic. Over time, the snow layers compacted into massive sheets of ice, and when the ice sheets began moving under the pressure of their own weight, they became glaciers. At their peak, massive glaciers thousands of feet thick covered nearly all of Canada and parts of the northern U.S.

COLORADO GLACIERS

North Park

Fort Collins

Estes Park

Lyons

Grand Lake

Boulder

Denver

Vail

Aspen

Mount Elbert

South Park

Pikes Peak

Crested Butte

Telluride

South Park

Durango

Although vast continental glaciers never reached as far south as Colorado, smaller glaciers formed in the Rocky Mountains. There have been at least three major glacial events in Colorado, the first starting around 1.6 million years ago. The two most recent events are the Bull Lake Glaciation and Pinedale Glaciation, which peaked around 140,000 years ago and 20,000 years ago respectively. During the Pinedale Glaciation, over half a dozen large glaciers formed in Rocky Mountain National Park. The largest, the Kawuneeche Glacier, stretched 20 miles and was over 2,000 feet thick.

As glaciers flowed through the park, they consumed everything in their path. Boulders, soil, trees—everything but the bedrock was picked up and carried along. But even the bedrock did not escape unscathed. The glaciers—essentially dirty ice full of debris—acted like giant sheets of sandpaper, grinding down the bedrock and smoothing it out.

The force of the glaciers was massive. Under the largest glaciers, pressures topped several hundred pounds per square inch. Where bedrock was weakened by cracks, glaciers plucked out large chunks of rock and carried them to lower elevations. Where bedrock was solid and relatively crack-free, glaciers smoothed out the rock and formed glacial polish—a glassy veneer polished to a shine. Rocks embedded at the bottom of the glacier sometimes scraped the glacial polish, creating long scratches called glacial striations.

Descending from high elevations at speeds ranging from several inches to several feet per day, glaciers flowed through previously formed V-shaped river valleys and gouged out their sides, creating broad U-shaped valleys. The glaciers acted like giant conveyor belts transporting loose debris to lower elevations. Debris deposited on the sides of the glaciers formed enormous landforms called lateral moraines. Today Moraine Park (p.133) showcases some of the finest lateral moraines in America. As glaciers descended to lower, warmer elevations, they melted. But flowing ice continued transporting debris to the front of the glaciers, forming terminal moraines that mark their maximum extent.

When global temperatures rose, melting glaciers often flooded the area between tall moraines and formed large lakes. Over time the lakes slowly filled with sediment and organic debris, and when the lakes drained or dried out they left large, flat meadows behind. Moraine Park and Horseshoe Park are two excellent examples of glacially formed meadows in Rocky Mountain National Park.

By about 10,000 years ago, earth's climate warmed and large glaciers disappeared from Rocky Mountain National Park. But global temperatures have continued to fluctuate, and there have been three minor glacial advances in the last 5,000 years. The most recent glacial advance occurred from A.D. 1200 to 1880 during a period of cooling called the Little Ice Age. The small glaciers that formed during the Little Ice Age shrank in the early 1900s, grew in the late-1900s, and have retreated slightly since.

The Rocky Mountains

Stretching 3,000 miles from British Columbia to New Mexico, the Rocky Mountains are the longest mountain range in North America and the second-longest mountain range in the world (after the Andes). The Continental Divide runs the length of the Rockies, forming the "backbone of America" and dividing most of the country into Atlantic and Pacific watersheds.

The origin of the name Rocky Mountains may have come from a native word that means "rocky mass." In 1752, Canadian explorer Jacques Legardeur de Saint-Pierre became the first European to formally record the *Montagnes de Roche*, "Mountains of Rock." The Rockies vary in width from 70 to 300 miles, and they are home to some of America's most spectacular national parks, including Yellowstone, Grand Teton, Glacier, and (of course) Rocky Mountain National Park.

Colorado boasts the highest peak in the Rockies, Mount Elbert, which towers 14,440 feet above sea level. It is the second-tallest mountain in the continental United States after Mount Whitney (14,505 feet) in California. Nearly all of the 100 highest peaks in the Rockies are located in Colorado, including every fourteener in the range. Roughly 75 percent of U.S. land above 10,000 feet lies within Colorado's boundaries. Not only is Colorado the highest state in America, but its average elevation (6,800 feet) is higher than North Carolina's Mount Mitchell (6,684 feet), the highest point east of the Mississippi.

Most of the world's mountain ranges form near coastlines where tectonic plates collide, crumpling the land and thrusting up mountains. The Rockies are highly unusual because they formed in the heart of a continent. They are also surrounded by two high provinces, the Great Plains and Colorado Plateau, which experienced little deformation—a geography unique among mountain ranges in the world. Geologists still struggle to understand how the Rocky Mountains formed. Despite decades of research, the Rockies remain one of the earth's most puzzling mountain ranges.

The Rocky Mountains supply about 25 percent of the water in the United States. Rivers born in the Rockies pass through some of the most arid regions in North America, and they are among the most litigated and contested rivers in the world. The Colorado Rockies receive up to 200 inches of snow each year, accounting for nearly 80 percent of the state's precipitation. Most snow falls on the western slope, but over 80 percent of Colorado's population lives east of the Rockies. Today a dozen water diversion projects send roughly 150 billion gallons of water across the Continental Divide each year. In Rocky Mountain National Park both the Grand Ditch (p.268) and Big Thompson Water Project (p.52) divert water to the thirsty eastern plains.

Hidden Glaciers

In the depths of the Ice Age, Longs Peak was surrounded by large glaciers. Today tiny Mills Glacier, located just above Chasm Lake (p.194), is the only glacier that still flows below the summit. But some geologists believe a "hidden" glacier may also exist on Longs Peak. So-called rock glaciers consist of loose rocks that slowly flow downhill over time, and they are found throughout the Rockies. Geologist Jon Achuff suspects many rock glaciers cover actual glaciers. He believes the Boulderfield below the north face of Longs Peak may cover a glacier over one mile long and hundreds of feet deep. If so, it could be the largest glacier in Colorado.

GEOLOGY TODAY

Rocky Mountain National Park currently shelters some of the southernmost glaciers in the Rockies. The southernmost, Arapaho Glacier, is located just 10 miles south of the park. There are six named glaciers in the park, all of which are cirque glaciers that occupy bowl-shaped basins scooped out by larger glaciers in the past. The park also contains over 20 permanent snowfields.

Current glaciers, which are significantly smaller than their Ice Age counterparts, generally cling to north- to east-facing slopes, which provide enough shade to keep them from melting. Most glaciers are perched just east of the Continental Divide, and all are sustained by snow that falls west of the divide and blows east over the crest. These glaciers are covered with firn, a layer of snow that has not been converted to ice, and when the firn melts during dry years it sometimes reveals the cracked blue ice of the underlying glacier.

Rocky Mountain National Park has several dozen mapped snowfields where patches of snow exist year-round. While less erosive than glaciers, snowfields still alter the landscape. Repeated melting and freezing breaks up rocks below the snowfields in a process called nivation. Repeated freeze-thaw cycles scoop out the landscape under the snow, creating concavities called nivation hollows.

Freeze-thaw cycles are one of the most powerful forces shaping the park today. When water freezes and expands in cracks it generates massive pressures—up to 20,000 pounds per square inch—that split rocks apart and trigger rockfalls. Rock climbers on Longs Peak have witnessed car-sized boulders fall from above. A 200-foot rock pillar is currently semi-detached from Longs Peak's sheer eastern face, and at some point it will topple. Freezing water can also shatter bedrock, leaving "fellfields" of jumbled rocks like those found on the summit of Longs Peak. In alpine tundra, freeze-thaw cycles bring buried rocks to the surface, creating "periglacial landforms" that form circles, polygons, and other unusual patterns on the ground.

Flooding is another powerful erosional force, and multiple floods have roared through the park over the past century. On the night of July 31, 1976, 12 inches of rain fell in four hours, causing the Big Thompson River to rise nearly 20 feet. The flood roared through Big Thompson Canyon and claimed 145 lives—the worst natural disaster in Colorado history. In 1982 the Lawn Lake Flood (p.227) originated high above Horseshoe Park and roared through downtown Estes Park.

Although not known for earthquakes, Colorado sits on numerous active faults. The state's largest known historic earthquake occurred in Estes Park on November 7, 1882. That powerful earthquake (estimated at 6.6 on the Richter scale) triggered rockfalls in the mountains, knocked out power in Denver, and was felt in Salt Lake City over 300 miles away. Estes Park has experienced smaller earthquakes since then—and it could experience larger ones in the future.

ECOLOGY

ROCKY MOUNTAIN NATIONAL PARK reveals some of the most fascinating ecosystems in America. The park's lowest elevations—which would be the *highest* elevations in many national parks—shelter idyllic meadows filled with deer, elk, and other wildlife. Trail Ridge Road rises thousands of feet above the meadows, passing majestic forests before twisting 11 spectacular miles above treeline. Roughly one-third of the park lies above the trees. This harsh and mysterious world, which includes the most dramatic expanse of alpine tundra in Colorado, is normally the domain of rugged mountain climbers. But in Rocky Mountain National Park anyone can explore this remarkable landscape.

And yet many visitors pass through the mountains unaware of the natural wonders that surround them. Visiting the park without a basic understanding of alpine ecology is like walking into one of the world's great libraries not knowing how to read. Learn a little about alpine plants and animals, and the Rockies come alive. Seemingly minor observations—a twisted tree here, a delicate wildflower there—become fascinating clues in a larger narrative that reveals the epic ecological story of Rocky Mountain National Park.

The story began about 20,000 years ago, when enormous Ice Age glaciers started to melt. Although glaciers once covered the highest elevations in the Rockies, they disappeared from Colorado around 10,000 years ago. In their place was a barren landscape of glistening rock polished clean by moving ice. It must have been a remarkable sight—silvery peaks, free of vegetation, towering above the flatlands. But the mountains did not stay barren for long.

Shortly after glaciers retreated, lichens colonized the rocks. Lichens consist of two primitive organisms: algae and fungus. The fungus provides physical habitat for the algae, and the algae photosynthesizes nutrients to feed the fungus. Working together, lichens scraped out a meager existence on rocks, growing as little as one millimeter per century. But over thousands of years they achieved remarkable things. The rough folds of lichen trapped tiny organic particles blown by the wind, and wet lichen released a weak acid that slowly broke down rocks. Eventually this produced a thin layer of soil where tundra plants like herbs and grasses could grow. These vascular plants further accelerated soil formation, adding new layers of organic matter that paved the way for larger plants.

Eventually, enough soil formed to support sun-loving trees, which thrived in the open, sunny landscape. Thinleaf alder was one of the first trees to colonize the mountains after glaciers departed, growing along creeks and contributing fallen leaves to soil. Aspen and lodgepole pines later took root, creating a shady forest that attracted Douglas-fir and Engelmann spruce seedlings, which thrived on the shady forest floor. Eventually, these shade-loving trees grew above the sun-loving trees, robbing them of sunlight and displacing them.

This ongoing process of new species colonization in response to changing conditions is called succession. In the long term, succession occurs as global climate fluctuates, pushing plant species to higher or lower elevations in response to changing temperatures. Between 11,000 and 7,000 years ago, conditions were warmer and drier than today, and plants migrated to higher, cooler elevations. When temperatures cooled around 5,000 years ago, small glaciers formed and plants migrated to lower, warmer elevations. By about 2,000 years ago, conditions became similar to the present-day Rockies.

In the short term, succession occurs when natural disturbances such as fire, avalanches, or insect infestations destroy vegetation. These disturbances are heavily influenced by climate. During cool, snowy periods, avalanches are more common. During warm, dry periods, wildfires increase. Following disturbances, sun-loving plants colonize open patches and the successional process starts again. Eventually so-called climax species dominate, remaining relatively unchanged, sometimes for centuries, until the next catastrophe.

Plants form the foundation of a healthy food chain. As a result, plant species largely determine the distribution of animals in Rocky Mountain National Park. Some ecosystems, like wetlands and aspen forests, support a wide range of animals. Others, like lodgepole pine forests, support relatively few. Because plants ripen at different elevations throughout the year, animals migrate between different ecological zones. Predators, in turn, follow their favorite prey.

Colorado's Front Range contains a striking abundance of plant and animal species. Rising 9,000 vertical feet over a relatively short distance, the Front Range compresses multiple ecological zones into a remarkably small area. In places it's less than 16 miles from shortgrass plains to alpine tundra. All told, the Front Range has an estimated 1,500 species of ferns, conifers, and flowering plants. Few regions in North America boast such impressive ecological diversity. In Rocky Mountain National Park alone there are over 60 mammal species, over 270 bird species, over 150 lichen species, and nearly 1,000 plant species.

The park has three major ecological zones: montane, subalpine, and alpine. Additional habitats, such as krummholz and mountain meadows, further diversify the landscape. The three major ecological zones are largely determined by elevation, and they often overlap along fuzzy boundaries called ecotones. Local microclimates, such as sunny warm southern slopes or shady cool northern slopes, often push ecological boundaries higher or lower.

Montane

Ranging from 5,600 to 9,500 feet in elevation, the montane ecosystem is the lowest and warmest part of the park. Moraine Park, Horseshoe Park, Upper Beaver Meadows, and Kawuneeche Valley are classic examples of this beautiful region. Gentle rivers and streams flow through lush meadows, and water-loving trees like willows and mountain alders grow along riverbanks. The meadows attract a wide range of wildlife. Mule deer and elk browse shrubs, small mammals feed on abundant grasses, and songbirds nibble on insects. Hawks perch in nearby trees looking for prey, including Wyoming ground squirrels, which burrow elaborate tunnels under the meadows. The montane ecosystem is also home to reptiles and amphibians, many of which are at the upper limit of their range. Most cold-blooded animals in the Rockies are unable to survive the colder temperatures at higher elevations.

Montane forests support four common tree species: ponderosa pines, Douglas-firs, lodgepole pines, and aspen. Ponderosa pines often grow on south-facing slopes, which tend to be sunny and dry. The trees are often spaced widely apart, creating ponderosa pine savannas. These are the warmest and driest ecological communities in the park. The open, sunny ponderosa savannas promote the growth of grass and shrubs, attracting more animals than any other forest type. Dozens of mammals feed on ponderosa seeds, including the tassel-eared Abert's squirrel, which lives exclusively in ponderosa forests. North-facing slopes, which tend to be shady and moist, support dark forests of Douglas-firs. Because few

animals eat Douglas-fir needles or bark, these forests support far fewer animals than meadows or ponderosa savannas. Aspen and lodgepole pines grow towards the upper limit of the montane zone, preferring sunny, open areas. Aspen also flourish along rivers, streams, and well-watered areas.

Subalpine

Shady forests of Engelmann spruce and subalpine fir dominate elevations above 9,000 feet. These trees, identified by their dark green color and narrow crowns, grow all the way to treeline 11,500 feet above sea level. Subalpine fir, the only true fir in Rocky Mountain National Park, has cones that grow upright like candles on a Christmas tree. Aspen and lodgepole pines often grow near the lower elevations of the subalpine zone in recently disturbed areas. Limber pines, named for incredibly flexible branches that evolved to cope with relentless winds, cling to rocky outcrops where conditions are too extreme for other trees.

Heavy snow makes the subalpine zone the wettest forest community in Colorado. In Silver Lake, Colorado, about 10 miles south of the park, a subalpine forest once received over six feet of snow in 24 hours, setting a U.S. record. In addition to direct snowfall, subalpine forests also catch snow blown down from higher elevations, increasing effective precipitation. Moisture is abundant in the subalpine zone, but late snowmelt and cold temperatures result in an extremely short growing season—less than two frost-free months in some places. These moist, chilly conditions offer some protection from wildfires. As a result, trees in the subalpine zone are among the oldest and largest in the park. The most common disturbances are avalanches, which topple spruce and fir and open sunny areas preferred by aspen and lodgepole pine seedlings. Due to the short growing season, succession takes much longer in the subalpine zone. It can sometimes take a century or more for Engelmann spruce and subalpine fir to reclaim their former territory.

Subalpine forests do not support a rich diversity of wildlife. Deep, lingering snows deter many animals, with the exception of well-adapted species like snowshoe hares. Most animals that live in the subalpine zone feed on spruce and fir seeds, including red squirrels, Clark's nutcrackers, mountain chickadees, and Steller's Jays. Elk visit in summer, escaping the heat and insects found at lower elevations. Bears, mountain lions, deer, and coyotes also pass through.

Krummholz

At the upper limit of treeline lies one of the park's most unusual ecological zones: the krummholz. This rugged habitat—the last outpost of tree life before survival becomes impossible—is easily identified by short, twisted trees. *Krummholz* is a German word that means "crooked wood." Trees here grow stout and twisted due to regular, hurricane-force winds. Some trees only have branches on their leeward side (away from prevailing winds) because high winds strip away all branches not protected by the trunk. Krummholz trees often cluster in small "tree islands" for additional wind protection. Over time, some tree islands migrate leeward as harsh conditions kill trees on the windward edge.

Summer temperatures determine the upper limit of tree life. Most trees can survive excruciatingly cold winters, but they cannot grow without a few warm weeks each summer. Krummholz trees in the park enjoy about two frost-free months a year. As a result, they grow far more slowly than normal. The park's most common krummholz trees—Engelmann spruce, subalpine pine, limber pine—can be hundreds of years old yet measure only a few feet tall. Many krummholz trees reproduce by growing roots from low-lying branches. After the roots are established, they grow into new tree trunks. This process, called layering, consumes far less energy than producing seeds.

Alpine

Above treeline lies the alpine zone—the most extreme environment in the park. Summer temperatures average about 50°F (10°C), and thin air does little to block intense UV radiation. In winter, temperatures drop to 40°F below zero (-40°C), and 100 mph winds roar across the landscape. Only the most rugged plants and animals can survive such harrowing conditions. In Rocky Mountain National Park most of the alpine zone is covered in alpine tundra, but there are also glaciers, permanent snowfields, and large expanses of barren rock.

Alpine Tundra

There's no better place in America to experience alpine tundra than Rocky Mountain National Park. This rugged land above the trees covers 89,000 acres in Rocky—nearly one third of the park's total area—and vast stretches are easily viewed along Trail Ridge Road. At first glance alpine tundra appears relatively barren. But look close and you'll discover a secret world of astonishing life forms. Their survival strategies are ingenious, their adaptations remarkable, and during summer blooms, which only last a few weeks, the rooftop of Rocky explodes in a brilliant kaleidoscope of miniature flowers.

The word *tundra* comes from the Sámi people of Scandinavia and Russia. It means "land of no trees," and today it describes both a type of vegetation and a specific ecosystem. Vast expanses of arctic tundra grow near sea level in northern Russia, Scandinavia, Alaska, and Canada. Alpine tundra, which constitutes 40 percent of all tundra in the Northern Hemisphere, grows on mountains above treeline. During the Ice Age, when continental glaciers pushed ecosystems hundreds of miles south, tundra colonized large parts of North America. Today tundra only survives below Canada on tall mountains. Colorado has more alpine tundra than any state besides Alaska, and Rocky Mountain National Park protects one of the largest expanses of alpine tundra in Colorado. There are more than 300 alpine tundra species in Colorado—double the number of West Coast species and triple the number of East Coast species.

Alpine tundra endures the most extreme climate in the park. Winter can last nine months or more, with freezing temperatures and relentless winds. Snow acts as a natural blanket, shielding tundra plants from scouring winds and maintaining ground temperatures just below freezing. Many plants retain green leaves throughout winter. This allows them to photosynthesize immediately after the snow melts.

Alpine tundra summer is a frost-free season that lasts roughly six weeks. It's an explosion of life, generally peaking in July, with plants rushing to reproduce before "autumn" arrives in August. The park boasts over 100 species of flowering tundra plants. To conserve energy, many plants bloom every other year. Others wait over two

years to bloom, and some reproduce asexually instead of expending energy to make seeds. Nearly all alpine tundra plants are perennials that use the same roots year after year. Root systems, which make up 90 percent of some plants, store nutrients below ground where conditions are less severe. This abundant stored energy helps plants survive winter and jumpstart the growing process as soon as snow melts.

Alpine Tundra Range

Most tundra plants grow low to the ground to avoid scouring winds. Dense hairs and waxy coatings offer additional protection from the elements. Above treeline sunlight is 25 percent brighter and ultraviolet rays are twice as strong as at sea level. Many tundra plants produce reddish/purple anthocyanin pigments that convert visible light into heat. In autumn when chlorophyll wanes, these plants turn bright red.

Alpine tundra often looks blandly uniform from a distance, but it's actually a rich mosaic of diverse plant communities. Half a dozen different communities can occupy a relatively small area. Where they grow is largely determined by lingering winter snow, which affects both moisture and sunlight. Even slight changes in topography can dramatically alter the timing of snowmelt. Purple Parry's clover and dwarf willow prefer shallow depressions that hold snow until early summer. Yellow snow buttercup prefer deeper depressions that hold snow even longer. Keen tundra observers can often tell how much snow covers the ground in winter simply by looking at the summer plants.

In summer and fall, alpine tundra attracts grazers including elk, mule deer, and bighorn sheep. Year-round residents include marmots, pika, and pocket gophers. Gophers dig extensive tunnels under tundra, aerating and fertilizing the soil. Just three animals are hardy enough to live year-round on alpine tundra without hibernating: bighorn sheep, foxes, and white-tailed ptarmigans.

One of the best places to experience alpine tundra is the Tundra Communities Trail (p.250) on Trail Ridge Road. Near the trailhead is a research plot where ecologist Beatrice Willard studied alpine tundra for decades. Her 1972 book, *The Land Above The Trees*, was the first comprehensive guide to alpine tundra in America. In 2007, her research plots became the first ever added to the National Register of Historic Places. As Willard wrote, "there is very much that 'grows above the trees.' But it takes close looking ... getting down on hands and knees—or even stomach—to examine a mini-forest at your toes."

Human Impact

Whether Paleo-Indians hunted large Ice Age animals to extinction is a matter of debate. Some archaeologists believe climate change played a decisive role. Later tribes hunted bison on foot, but after acquiring horses in the 1600s they became ruthlessly efficient hunters. Bison, which once gathered by the millions on the plains, were largely absent along the Front Range when white settlers arrived. By that point beaver had also been depleted by both white and native trappers.

Early settlers in Estes Park hunted abundant game for sport and profit. Within a few decades, however, grizzly bears and wolves were gone. The removal of top predators, particularly wolves, altered the local ecology. Elk, which were extirpated in the late 1800s and reintroduced in 1913, exploded in population. By the 1990s there were as many as 285 elk per square mile in Moraine Park—the highest concentration ever recorded in the wild. This led to severe overgrazing of grasslands, willows, and aspen, reducing habitat for dozens of animals, most notably beavers. Today the park manages elk populations through a combination of methods, including fencing off fragile vegetation.

A lack of predators also paved the way for what is now the largest animal in the park: moose. When wolves and grizzlies flourished, moose were rare. In 1978, Colorado reintroduced 24 moose to North Park, some of which migrated into Kawuneeche Valley in Rocky Mountain National Park. Today there are several dozen moose throughout the park.

Forests also experienced profound changes, both in and outside the park. In the drought-prone West, trees evolved with fire. Small fires play an important role in forest ecosystems, clearing out debris, recycling nutrients, killing pests, and diversifying habitats. Large trees are often protected by thick, fire-resistant bark, and species like aspen and lodgepole pines thrive in a fire's wake. Lodgepole pines actually require hot temperatures to open cones and release seeds.

Throughout much of the 20th century, however, government agencies pursued a policy of fire suppression. In the absence of small fires, debris accumulated on the forest floor. This created the potential for larger, more destructive fires that could kill mature trees. Although the park suppresses human-caused fires, since 1971 small lightening-ignited fires are sometimes allowed to burn. These closely monitored fires reduce debris and help return forests to a more natural state. The park also conducts prescribed fires, burning dead trees and other fuels under tightly controlled conditions.

As temperatures increased over the past few decades, so did the risk of large, intense fires in Rocky Mountain National Park. In addition to creating dry, tinderbox conditions, warm temperatures led to outbreaks of mountain pine beetles (right), which killed hundreds of thousands of trees, littering the forests like matches. All of these factors contributed to the outbreak of the two largest fires in Colorado history, which swept through the park in 2020 (p.130).

Mountain Pine Beetle
Dendroctonus ponderosae

These tiny beetles are roughly the size of a grain of rice, but they have ravaged forests throughout the West, including those in Rocky Mountain National Park. Hundreds of thousands of dead gray trees stand like tombstones in the park, marking the beetle's destructive path. The current outbreak, which began in 2002, is the most severe on record, affecting over 90 percent of park forest. And yet these miniature tree terrorists are among the most fascinating creatures in the Rockies.

Mountain pine beetles are native to western North America. Under normal circumstances they are part of a healthy forest ecosystem, infesting and killing large, susceptible trees. This opens up old forests, encouraging the growth of healthy new trees. Mountain pine beetles infest about a dozen different tree species, including lodgepole and ponderosa pines. In summer thousands of beetles attack the same tree in unison, boring holes to reach the tree's succulent phloem tissue that transports water and nutrients. Beetles also carry a blue-stain fungus that weakens the tree's defenses. Females lay up to 200 eggs in tiny tunnels, and after hatching the larvae feast on phloem, which further weakens the tree. The following summer mature beetles abandon the dying tree and fly to new trees, repeating the cycle.

Healthy trees attempt to repel attacking beetles by pushing them out with pitch, but trees lacking sufficient moisture cannot produce enough pitch. When beetles invade a weakened tree, the beetles release powerful pheromones to attract even more beetles. This onslaught overwhelms a tree's defenses, at which point the victorious beetles release a new pheromone to deter new arrivals. By limiting the total number of beetles, the invaders ensure sufficient phloem for developing larvae.

Beetle larvae survive subzero temperatures by eliminating liquids from their body, preventing the formation of deadly ice crystals. They also produce glycerol and polyhydric alcohols that act as natural antifreeze. Beetle larvae can survive temperatures as low as -20°F for short periods of time, but they cannot survive extended cold spells. For centuries, cold winter temperatures kept mountain pine beetle populations in check. But warming temperatures and multi-year droughts have weakened

Mountain Pine Beetle Outbreak

millions of trees, resulting in massive beetle outbreaks across the West. Although woodpeckers feast on mountain pine beetles, they cannot control their numbers. The current beetle outbreak, which stretches from Canada to Mexico (left), is believed to be the largest in centuries.

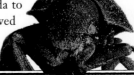

Colorado Blue Columbine
Aquilegia coerulea

Showy Milkweed
Asclepias speciosa

Fireweed
Chamaenerion angustifolium

Rocky Mountain Penstemon
Penstemon strictus

Common Blanketflower
Gaillardia aristata

American Bistort
Bistorta bistortoides

Narrowleaf Paintbrush
Castilleja linariifolia

Woods' Rose
Rosa woodsii

Gunnison's Mariposa Lily
Calochortus gunnisonii

Whipple's Penstemon
Penstemon whippleanus

Elephant's head
Pedicularis groenlandica

Parry's Clover
Trifolium parryi

Quaking Aspen
Populus tremuloides

Quaking aspen are among the most beautiful trees in the park, particularly in autumn, when the mountains shimmer in gold. Aspen have the widest range of any tree in North America, spanning 47 degrees of latitude (over half the distance from the equator to the North Pole), 110 degrees of longitude (from Alaska to Newfoundland), and elevations ranging from sea level to 12,000 feet. In Rocky Mountain National Park, aspen generally grow between 8,000 and 10,000 feet. At higher elevations they often grow on sunny, south-facing slopes. Many trees are less than 50 feet tall, but they can grow as high as 130 feet. Aspen bark, which appears bright white, is actually slightly green and can photosynthesize. Aspen leaves attach to branches via long stems called petioles, and they tremble and quake at the slightest breeze, hence the name quaking aspen. This could be an evolutionary adaptation to withstand strong winds, and it may even allow more sunlight to reach the photosynthetic bark. Sun-loving aspen grow quickly in the wake of forest fires, improving soil quality and encouraging a rich, herbaceous understory that supports a wide range of animals. Deer and elk eat the bark, twigs, and leaves. Unfortunately, overgrazing by elk has left many aspen in the park with scarred and blackened trunks near ground level. Aspen produce tiny seeds with silky hairs, but they frequently reproduce through root sprouts, called suckers, which are clones of the original tree. Although individual trees often live less than 150 years, root systems can live for thousands of years. The world's largest known aspen clone, located in Utah, has 47,000 stems, covers over 100 acres, and is estimated to weigh over 13 million pounds. It is considered the world's oldest and largest land organism.

Ponderosa Pine

Pinus ponderosa

Ponderosa pines are the largest conifer species in Rocky Mountain National Park. They are easily identified by their height (up to 150 feet tall), long needles (up to eight inches in bundles of three), and thick, plate-like bark. They generally grow below 9,500 feet in the park. Ponderosa pines are the most widely distributed pine species in North America. Their range stretches from Canada to Mexico, and they are found in every U.S. Western state. The tree is named for its heavy wood (*ponderosa* is Spanish for "heavy"), which is prized as lumber. Ponderosa roots spread up to 100 feet laterally, providing a sturdy base for the large, heavy trees. Ponderosa bark is famous because it smells like vanilla or butterscotch, particularly on hot days. Utes chewed on the inner bark for its sweet flavor, and they sometimes ate it as emergency food. Ponderosa savannahs are among the most biodiverse ecosystems in the park, but the warm, dry savannahs are also among the most fire-prone. Ponderosa pines can survive low-intensity fires thanks to thick bark, and mature trees are sometimes charred near the base. Small fires clear out competing species that would otherwise encroach on ponderosa habitat. Only large fires that burn the crown can kill a mature ponderosa. Older trees often drop lower branches to prevent fire from climbing the tree and reaching the vulnerable crown. Ponderosas can even survive lightning strikes, which flash-boil the sap and blow off chunks of bark, sending energy away from the tree. Under ideal conditions ponderosa pines can live 600 years or longer.

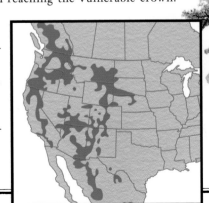

Douglas-Fir

Pseudotsuga menziesii

Douglas-fir forests cover shady, north-facing slopes below 9,000 feet in Rocky Mountain National Park. At higher elevations they tend to grow on warmer, south-facing slopes, and a few hardy stragglers survive near treeline. Rocky Mountain Douglas-firs rarely grow taller than 100 feet, but coastal Douglas fir, a related variety in the Pacific Northwest, grows up to 300 feet tall. Both varieties are easily identified by their pine cones (1.5 to 3 inches long), which feature unusual lobed bracts protruding from the scales. Some people compare the bracts to the forked tongue of a snake. Others, including some native tribes, see the hindquarters of a mouse trying to climb into the cone. When mature cones dry out, papery winged seeds disperse on the wind. Douglas-fir are named after David Douglas, a Scottish botanist who studied the tree in the 1820s. Douglas-fir is not a true fir, which is why its name is hyphenated. True firs have upright cones and rounded buds. Douglas-firs have hanging cones and pointed buds. Rocky Mountain Douglas-fir has the largest north-south range of any conifer in North America, stretching from British Columbia to the mountains of southern Mexico. It has an extra pair of chromosomes not found in any other pine species, and it thrives in a wide range of environments thanks to diverse genotypes. Douglas-fir forests tend to be cool, shady places with limited sunlight. Mature trees have thick, cork-like bark that protects them from ground fires, but dense forests are highly susceptible to crown fires. Early settlers prized Douglas-fir for its strength—it has a higher strength-to-weight ratio than steel—and large stands were harvested throughout Colorado. Today Douglas-fir is grown and harvested on six continents.

Coastal Douglas-fir
Rocky Mountain Douglas-fir

Lodgepole Pine
Pinus contorta

Found at elevations between 7,800 and 11,500 feet in the park, lodgepole pines have gently rounded treetops, yellow-green foliage, and a thin, cornflake-like bark. They grow up to 90 feet tall, and their two-inch-long pine needles grow in bundles of two. Native tribes used the famously straight lodgepoles for the poles of their lodges (tipis). Colorado is the southern limit of the lodgepole subspecies that grows in the Rockies. Lodgepole forests are among the least diverse ecosystems in the park. They are typically cool, shady places that tend to be quiet, although chattering chickarees occasionally pierce the silence. Lodgepoles are the most fire-adapted trees in the Rocky Mountains. Their cones, which can survive on branches for decades, require extremely hot temperatures to melt their resinous coatings, which triggers the release of seeds. This typically occurs during a fire, and lodgepole seedlings flourish on the bare mineral soil left in a fire's wake. Seedlings require abundant sunlight. They cannot tolerate shade, so only the tallest, fastest growing seedlings survive. Lower branches often drop off as lodgepoles grow taller, giving trees a stick-like appearance. Some mature lodgepole forests are so consistently spaced they could be mistaken for a tree farm. But mature forests block so much sun that young lodgepoles cannot grow. As a result, shade-loving species like Douglas-fir, Engelmann spruce, and subalpine fir colonize lodgepole forests. Over time these species grow taller than lodgepoles, robbing them of sunlight and replacing them as a climax species. Lodgepole forests can only perpetuate if new, sunny spaces are created through fire, avalanches, or other disturbances. In recent years mountain pine beetles have killed millions of lodgepoles, leaving dead trees scattered throughout the mountains.

Limber Pine
Pinus flexilis

Limber pines grow across the West, but they are most prominent in southern Wyoming and northern Colorado, where they dominate exposed sites near treeline. Long taproots anchor the trees to steep cliffs and rocky outcrops. Flexible branches, which give the tree its common name, evolved to cope with relentless mountain winds. These adaptations allow limber pines to thrive in locations where other trees would die. Near treeline, strong winds twist limber pines into bizarre, gnarled shapes, and some trees grow as wide as they are tall. Their range extends as low as 7,000 feet in elevation, where limber pines can sometimes grow up to 50 feet tall. Their needles come in bundles of five, and cones produce large nuts eaten by squirrels, bears, and birds. Clark's nutcrackers play a major role in the limber pine's life cycle. The birds extract seeds from limber pine cones with long, sturdy bills, then bury the seeds in caches up to several miles away from the tree. Seeds from forgotten caches grow into new trees. Multiple seedlings often grow closely together, and sometimes their stems twist together and fuse at the base. Limber pines are often the first trees to grow in recently burned areas. They are important colonizers, stabilizing soil and creating a shady canopy that attracts shade-loving tree species. Where only limber pines grow, they can live 1,000 years or longer. The oldest limber pine in Colorado is over 1,500 years old. Today the tree's greatest threat is white pine blister rust, an invasive fungus from Asia. The first case was discovered in Rocky Mountain National Park

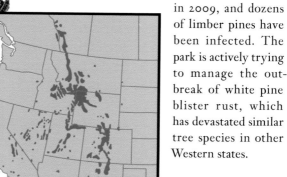

in 2009, and dozens of limber pines have been infected. The park is actively trying to manage the outbreak of white pine blister rust, which has devastated similar tree species in other Western states.

Engelmann Spruce

Picea engelmannii

Engelmann Spruce is one of two tree species that dominate the park's subalpine zone. The other is subalpine fir (*Abies lasiocarpa*), which is the only true fir in the park. Both spruce and fir are conifers with pine needles that attach to twigs individually, not in bunches like pines. But spruce have prickly, square needles that you can roll between your fingers. Fir needles are flat and soft to the touch, hence the phrase "friendly as a fir." Engelmann spruce grow above 9,000 feet in elevation, and their range extends to treeline. They are identified by narrow, spire-like crowns and downward-drooping cones that cluster near the top of the tree. Cones are one to two inches long with papery scales. Engelmann spruce are one of the few tree species that can reproduce in shade at high altitudes. Seedlings grow slowly, but mature trees can reach heights of 100 feet or more. Engelmann spruce grow in areas that are high, cold, and wet, so forest fires are infrequent. Many subalpine forests have not burned in centuries, and they contain some of the oldest trees in the park. When fire, avalanche, or insect pests remove Engelmann spruce, sun-loving lodgepole or aspen quickly invade the landscape. Once a shady canopy has developed, Engelmann spruce slowly reclaim their former territory, eventually dominating as a climax species. The Engelmann spruce beetle is the tree's most dangerous insect pest. Beetle populations are generally kept in check by woodpeckers, and recently burned Engelmann forests are some of the best places to look for three-toed woodpeckers. The Western spruce budworm, a small caterpillar that feeds on foliage, pollen, and buds, sometimes causes enough defoliation to kill mature trees. Engelmann spruce is considered an excellent tone wood, highly valued for making acoustic guitars, violins, and piano tops.

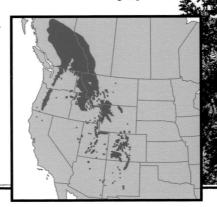

Golden Eagle
Aquila chrysaetos

With wingspans nearly seven feet across, golden eagles are roughly the same size as bald eagles—the largest birds of prey in North America. Their lethal combination of speed, power, and agility makes golden eagles among the park's deadliest predators. After spotting prey from the air, they swoop down at speeds topping 150 mph, clutching victims with talons so strong they can crush backbones. Common prey include rabbits, marmots, and squirrels, but golden eagles sometimes snatch mule deer fawns and bighorn sheep lambs. Golden eagles are named for the golden-brown napes on the back of their necks. Adults can weigh over 11 pounds and live over 30 years in the wild. Their range stretches across much of the Northern Hemisphere, making them the most widely distributed eagle species in the world. The American golden eagle (*Aquila chrysaetos canadensis*), a North American subspecies, ranges from Alaska to central Mexico.

Great Horned Owl
Bubo virginianus

Ranging from Alaska to Argentina, great horned owls are large birds of prey with wingspans up to five feet across. Their "horns" are prominent black and brown ear tufts. Large yellow eyes have exceptional night vision, and great horned owls rotate their head up to 270 degrees while scanning for prey. Natural-colored plumage camouflages owls while they rest in trees during the day. At night they hunt small rodents, rabbits, and birds, flying from perch to perch, then silently swooping down and crushing victims with powerful talons. Great horned owls often swallow prey whole, then regurgitate indigestible bone "pellets." When prey is too large to swallow, the owl uses its powerful, sharp beak to dismember victims. Occasionally great horned owls attack porcupines, often with fatal results for both animals.

Red-tailed Hawk
Buteo jamaicensis

Named for their russet red tail feathers, red-tailed hawks are the most common large hawks in North America, ranging from Alaska to the Caribbean. Its species name, *jamaicensis*, is derived from Jamaica, where naturalists first described the bird. Their shrill, 2- to 3-second scream is instantly recognizable from Hollywood movies, where it's frequently used (inaccurately) for eagles and other birds of prey. Red-tailed hawks are remarkably agile predators. They are one of the few birds capable of "kiting"— holding still against the wind like a kite on a string. Their eyes are eight times as powerful as human eyes, and after spotting prey they dive-bomb victims at speeds topping 120 mph. Powerful talons exert pressures up to 200 pounds per square inch. Up to 90 percent of their diet is small rodents, but they also eat rabbits, birds, and lizards. Although sometimes called "chickenhawks," red-tailed hawks rarely prey on chickens. Females are about 25 percent heavier than males, weighing up to 4.5 pounds. The largest red-tailed hawks have wingspans nearly five feet across. Adults live 20 years or longer in the wild, and pairs often mate for life. Red-tailed hawks lay eggs and raise chicks in large nests up to 75 feet off the ground.

Three-toed Woodpecker
Picoides dorsalis

Three-toed woodpeckers are one of five woodpecker species in Rocky Mountain National Park. They are identified by three toes (most woodpeckers have four), black wings, white breasts, and white stripes under their eyes. Males have bright yellow patches on top of their heads, as do both male and female juveniles. Adults grow up to eight inches long. Three-toed woodpeckers are often found in recently burned conifer forests and areas with large bark beetle outbreaks. Bark beetles constitute the majority of their diet, and woodpeckers play an important role in controlling spruce bark beetle populations. Mating woodpeckers excavate nest cavities in dead conifers. They line the nest with excavated wood chips. Three-toed woodpeckers breed farther north than any other American woodpecker. Their range, which covers much of Alaska and Canada, extends down the Rocky Mountains as far south as New Mexico.

Wild Turkey
Meleagris gallopavo

Wild turkeys are the same species as domestic turkeys cooked at Thanksgiving, but wild turkeys are divided into six subspecies. They often travel in large flocks while searching for nuts, berries, and insects. In spring, males puff out their tail feathers, swell their face wattles, and strut and gobble to attract females. Adult turkeys, which weigh 20 pounds or more, are among the heaviest birds in North America. They were domesticated in Mexico around A.D. 500, then sent to Europe by the Spanish in the early 1500s. The English word "turkey" is likely derived from the country Turkey, which exported the birds to England. Prior to colonization there were an estimated ten million wild turkeys in America. Hunting and habitat loss reduced populations to perhaps 200,000—a 98 percent decline—by the early 20th century. Wild turkey populations have since rebounded to over six million birds.

White-tailed Ptarmigan
Lagopus leucura

White-tailed ptarmigans are the only birds that live year-round above treeline. Mottled summer plumage offers exceptional camouflage in alpine tundra, and snow-white winter plumage offers equally exceptional camouflage in snow. When temperatures drop, ptarmigan grow bristly projections on their feet, called pectinations, that act like natural snowshoes. Dense plumage and feathered feet help ptarmigans stay warm. In winter, ptarmigans burrow in snowbanks, often near willow thickets. Willow buds offer nutrient-rich food that keep ptarmigans plump throughout winter. When temperatures rise, their foot pectinations fall off and the birds spend the short summer gorging on plants, berries, and insects found on alpine tundra. Ptarmigan are monogamous, and pairs often mate for life. At the end of breeding season pairs separate, and females raise the chicks alone.

Black-billed Magpie
Pica hudsonia

Black-billed magpies are black and white birds distinguished by iridescent blue-green feathers on their wings and tail. Their range extends across much of the West, extending as far north as southern Alaska. Black-billed magpies often travel in groups, and they are sometimes seen along roads in the park's lower elevations. White wing tips are conspicuous when they fly. At night, large flocks often roost in ponderosa pine forests. At dawn, black-billed magpies often migrate to the eastern plains, foraging all day and returning to the mountains at dusk. Their omnivorous diet includes insects, nuts, fruit, nuts, small animals, and carrion. Black-billed magpies sometimes pluck ticks from the backs of deer, elk, and moose.

Mountain Chickadee
Poecile gambeli

These tiny birds, which only weigh half an ounce, need just 10 calories a day to survive. Their diet includes bark beetles in summer and conifer seeds in winter. Happiest in dry conifer forests, their range covers much of the mountain West and extends as far north as Yukon. A white stripe over the eye distinguishes mountain chickadees from all other chickadees. Their melodic call sounds like *chick-adee-dee-dee.*

Hummingbirds

There are four hummingbird species in the park: the broad-tailed hummingbird (right), ruby-throated hummingbird, rufus hummingbird, and calliope hummingbird. These tiny, iridescent birds hover in place and fly backwards, which helps them consume nectar from flowers. Their exceptional range of motion, unique among birds, is made possible by rotation of the entire wing at the shoulder joint. Most hummingbirds flap their wings dozens of times per second. To conserve energy at night, hummingbirds enter a state of "torpor," lowering their body temperature and heartbeat in a manner similar to hibernation.

Steller's Jay
Cyanocitta stelleri

These lovely blue birds range from Alaska to Nicaragua. In the western U.S. they are normally found at high elevations. Closely related to blue jays, Steller's jays are distinguished by black heads and black upper bodies. Their call is a harsh, descending *shaaaar*. Steller's jays also imitate the cries of predators such as red-tailed hawks, a trick they use to scare away other birds from feeding areas. Along with crows and magpies, jays are considered among the world's most intelligent birds. They are generally bold and inquisitive. Steller's jays eat pine nuts, fruits, seeds, insects, bird eggs, and even young birds. They are preyed upon, in turn, by goshawks, which snatch them with vice-like talons. Steller's jays, which often gather in flocks of 10 or more, live in Rocky Mountain National Park year-round. They are named after the German naturalist Georg Steller, who first recorded them in 1741.

Clark's Nutcracker
Nucifraga columbiana

Named after William Clark, of the Lewis and Clark expedition, these pale gray birds live in coniferous forests across western North America. Black wings have white patches along the trailing edges, and long, dagger-like bills extract pine seeds (nuts) from cones. Nutcrackers inspect seeds by shaking them in their bills, listening for a satisfying rattle. Seeds that pass the quality test are stored in a pouch under the nutcracker's tongue that can hold up to 50 seeds. Nutcrackers harvest tens of thousands of seeds each season, burying them in caches to provide food throughout winter. Clark's nutcrackers have extraordinary spatial memories, and they can remember the exact locations of hundreds of caches. Not all caches are retrieved, however, and forgotten seeds grow into new pine trees. As a result, nutcrackers play an important role in the life cycles of several pine species. Limber pines are a favorite of nutcrackers in Rocky Mountain National Park. Nutcrackers disperse large, wingless limber pine seeds over relatively large areas, and seeds buried several inches underground are often more likely to germinate than seeds that simply fall on the ground.

Western Tanager
Piranga ludoviciana

Members of the cardinal family, western tanagers are famous for the male's vibrant breeding plumage: a bright red face and yellow breast, which contrast with dark black wings. The red color comes from the pigment rhodoxanthin, which the birds likely acquire from insects that feed on pigment-producing plants. Females are far less showy, with a drab olive coloration. Like all cardinals western tanagers are classified as songbirds. Their call has been described as a hoarse, monotonous *pit-er-ick*. Their summer breeding range, which extends from Alaska to Mexico, covers much of western North America. Western tanagers build flimsy cup nests in which they typically lay four bluish-green eggs with brown spots. Their nests are preyed upon by Clark's nutcrackers and Steller's jays. Adult tanagers are preyed upon by hawks and falcons. The western tanager's winter range extends from central Mexico to Costa Rica, where they are often seen in coffee plantations. Sometimes they migrate alone, and sometimes they migrate in groups of up to 30 birds. The majority of their diet consists of insects, but they also feed on berries and fruits.

American Dipper
Cinclus mexicanus

American dippers, sometimes called ouzels, are the only songbirds in America that spend most of their time in and around water. In Rocky Mountain National Park these all-gray birds often perch on rocks in rushing streams. American dippers can dive up to 20 feet underwater and stay submerged for 30 seconds or longer. While underwater, they use their wings to swim in search of insects, larvae, and small fish. An extra eyelid allows American dippers to see underwater. The name "dipper" comes from the bird's habit of bouncing up and down on river rocks. Some scientists believe dipping is a form of communication that developed because bird calls are difficult to hear over the sound of rushing water. To survive cold water in winter, dippers have low metabolic rates and extra oxygen-carrying capacity in their blood. American dippers are found in streams and rivers across much of the mountain West. They sometimes build nests made of moss and twigs behind waterfalls, gaining access to the nest by flying through the waterfall.

Bighorn Sheep
Ovis canadensis

Bighorn sheep are the symbol of Rocky Mountain National Park and the state animal of Colorado, which has more bighorns than any other state in America. Exquisitely adapted to rugged, high-elevation terrain, bighorn sheep are among the most impressive animals in the park. Adult males weigh over 300 pounds, yet they navigate ledges two inches wide, scramble uphill at 15 mph, and jump down 20-foot inclines with grace. Concave hooves, which feature a hard outer edge and soft interior sole, help bighorns grip rocks on sheer cliffs and steep terrain. Their extraordinary agility, combined with keen eyesight, excellent hearing, and sharp sense of smell, help bighorns avoid predators such as mountain lions and coyotes. Wolves and grizzly bears also prey on bighorns, but those predators have not roamed the park in decades.

Rocky Mountain bighorn sheep are the largest wild sheep in North America. They are one of seven bighorn subspecies, and their range extends across the Rocky Mountains from British Columbia to New Mexico. In summer they have thin coats similar to desert bighorn sheep. In winter Rocky Mountain bighorns grow thick, double-layered coats to stay warm. Bighorn sheep are the only large grazers that live above treeline year-round, scratching through snow to nibble on dormant plants. Grasses constitute the majority of their diet, and shrubs provide additional calories. Bighorns have four stomachs and a complex nine-stage digestive process that extracts maximum nutrients from food.

Both males (rams) and females (ewes) develop horns shortly after birth. The horns grow larger each year, and annual growth rings indicate a bighorn sheep's age.

Ewe horns never grow past half curl, but ram horns curve up and over the ears in a dramatic C-shaped curl. A mature ram's horns can weigh up to 30 pounds—more than all other bones in its body combined—and measure three feet long. If horns start to block peripheral vision they are deliberately "broomed" (rubbed down) on rocks. During mating season, competing rams charge each other head-on at speeds topping 20 mph. When rams collide, their horns smash together, producing a loud crack like a rifle shot that can be heard over a mile away. Thickened skulls allow rams to withstand repeated collisions. Rams sometimes fight for over 24 hours, and aggressive rams with the biggest horns generally do the most mating. Although rams are independent by nature, they range between herds of ewes during mating season. Rams employ three major mating strategies: fighting rams for access to ewes, defending a single ewe in heat, and moving ewes away from competing rams.

Ewes leave their herd when it's time to give birth in spring. They climb to remote ledges that offer protection from most predators, but they must still guard against golden eagles swooping down and snatching lambs. After several days, when the lamb is old enough to walk, mother and child return to the herd. Within a few weeks, lambs separate from their mothers, seeking them out only to suckle. By six months, lambs are completely weaned. Lambs remain vulnerable to predation, however, and only one-quarter of bighorns survive their first year. Lambs that survive to adulthood often live 10 or more years in the wild. Males leave their mother's natal herd after two to four years, forming independent bachelor groups. Ewes stay with their natal herd for life.

Before European colonization, millions of bighorn sheep roamed North America, including an estimated 4,000 bighorns near Rocky Mountain National Park. But early settlers overhunted those herds, and Colorado declared bighorn sheep a protected species in 1885. When Rocky Mountain National Park was established in 1915, there were an estimated 1,000 bighorn sheep within its boundaries. By the 1960s, that number had dropped to just 150 bighorns. The drop was largely the result of diseases transmitted by domestic sheep grazing outside the park. Bighorns are gregarious by nature, and they often approach domestic sheep and touch noses, which transmits lethal bacteria and viruses.

In the late 1970s, wildlife managers reintroduced bighorn sheep to parts of their historic range. Since then, populations have slightly recovered in Rocky Mountain National Park. Today there are roughly 300–400 bighorn sheep divided into three major herds that roam the Mummy Range, the Continental Divide, and the Never Summer Mountains. Sheep Lakes (p.222) and Rock Cut (p.249) are two of the best places to look for bighorn sheep in the park.

Bighorn Lamb

Elk
Cervus canadensis

Elk are among the most majestic animals in Rocky Mountain National Park. Females (cows) grow up to seven feet long and weigh up to 500 pounds, while males (bulls) grow up to eight feet long and weigh over 1,000 pounds. Elk are similar in appearance to mule deer, but they are physically larger, with a dark brown "pelage" (coat) above the neck. Shawnee Indians call elk *wapiti*, "white rump," because of their white backsides.

Bulls have large antlers that can grow four feet long and weigh up to 40 pounds. They shed their antlers each spring, and over the next three to four months new antlers grow back at the rate of about one-half inch per day, reaching maximum size in time for the autumn rut. During the rut, bulls emit a bugle-like sound as a sign of dominance and a challenge to other bulls. The bugle starts off as a bellow and changes to a shrill scream that can be heard for miles. Dominance is determined through antler clashes, and dominant bulls assemble a harem of a dozen or more cows. To attract cows, bulls perfume themselves with their own urine. After a gestation period of roughly eight months, cows give birth to 30-pound newborns. Elk calves can stand within 20 minutes of birth, and they remain under their mothers's guidance for a full year. Those that survive to adulthood can live 10 years or more in the wild.

Elk are ruminants with four-chambered stomachs. They feed on grasses, leaves, twigs, buds, and bark. Elk roam the park in search of seasonal food, wandering alpine tundra in summer and gathering in montane meadows in fall and winter. When settlers first arrived in Estes Park, elk were abundant, but hunting led to a population crash by the late 1800s. In 1913, several dozen elk from Yellowstone were reintroduced to Rocky Mountain National Park. By that point, however, elk predators had also been overhunted, and elk populations exploded. By the 1940s, roughly 1,500 elk were overgrazing vegetation. Today the park manages its large elk population through a combination of methods, most notably fencing off fragile vegetation.

Mule Deer
Odocoileus hemionus

Mule deer often graze in meadows near the park's east entrance in early morning or late afternoon. The name mule deer is a reference to their large ears, which move independently of one another like the ears of a mule. Common throughout the West, their range extends from western Canada to central Mexico. Females (does) weigh 95 to 200 pounds, while males (bucks) weigh 150 to 300 pounds.

Mule deer are slightly larger than white-tailed deer, to which they are closely related. Mule deer have white tails with a black tip, and their bifurcated antlers "fork" as they grow. (The antlers of white-tailed deer, by contrast, branch from a single main beam.) Bucks grow a large pair of antlers each year, then shed them each winter. This annual cycle of antler growth is regulated by changes in the length of the day. Bucks compete for females during the autumn rut, enmeshing their antlers and trying to force the head of the other buck down. Injuries are rare, but antlers sometimes become locked together. If two bucks cannot unlock their antlers to feed, both will die of starvation. Mule deer forage plants, leaves, buds, and brushy vegetation. Like other ruminants, they have multi-chamber stomachs that ferment plants before digestion.

After breeding in autumn, gestation lasts roughly six and a half months. Young does give birth to one fawn, while older does often give birth to twins. Fawns are born with white spots to help camouflage them with the dappled light of the forest floor. As they grow older, the spots disappear. Fawns can identify their mother through a unique odor produced by glands on the mother's hind legs. Does live in multi-generational families, while bucks leave after one year to form their own independent groups. In autumn, mixed family groups often come together for protection, then split into smaller groups the following spring. Adults can live 11 years or more in the wild.

Mule deer were overhunted throughout Colorado in the late 1800s, and in 1913 the state enacted a hunting ban. Following the extirpation of wolves and grizzly bears, deer populations have made a steady comeback.

Black Bear

Ursus americanus

Black bears are rarely seen in Rocky Mountain National Park, but they are the most common bear species in North America. There are nearly one million black bears in the U.S. and Canada. Of North America's three bear species—black, grizzly, and polar—black bears are the smallest. They grow up to six feet long and weigh 600 pounds. Despite their roly-poly appearance, black bears can reach top speeds of 30 mph over short distances. They are also excellent tree climbers.

Black bears are highly intelligent, and their sense of smell is roughly 100 times more powerful than a dog's. Opportunistic omnivores, black bears eat just about anything: grass in spring, berries in summer, and pine seeds in autumn. Roughly 80 percent of their diet is vegetation, but bears also eat ants, termites, and insect larvae. Black bears have a particular fondness for human trash, which is why bear-proof trash cans are found throughout the park.

In autumn, black bears consume up to 20,000 calories per day in preparation for winter "hibernation." But black bears are not true hibernators. After snuggling into their dens in October or November, black bears enter a "light" hibernation referred to as seasonal lethargy. During this time, black bear heartbeats drop from roughly 70 beats per minute to as low as eight beats per minute. Compared to true hibernators, black bear body temperatures drop relatively little. During winter dormancy, which lasts three to five months, black bears lose roughly 25–30 percent of their total body weight.

Between the ages of three and five, females produce their first offspring. They breed about every two years after that. Mating season peaks in May and June, but embryos don't develop until autumn, when mothers have put on adequate weight to survive winter. Mothers give birth in the den after a two- to three-month gestation. Most litters consist of one to three cubs, which weigh less than a pound at birth. Youngsters stay with their mother throughout their first year while learning how to fend for themselves. Black bears live about 20 years in the wild.

Moose
Alces alces

Weighing up to 1,800 pounds, moose are the largest animals in Rocky Mountain National Park. Some moose stand 7.5 feet tall at the shoulder, and the tips of their antlers can tower 10 feet above ground. Despite their size, moose are surprisingly nimble. They can run up to 35 mph—nearly as fast as a deer—and swim up to six mph. Their long, gangly legs are well-adapted to walking through deep snow.

Moose are solitary animals that do not form herds. Males (bulls) are distinguished by massive antlers, which can stretch six feet across and weigh nearly 80 pounds. Antlers start growing in spring and are shed by December. They grow progressively larger each year until a bull reaches about five years in age. Antlers are used to mark territory, dig plants from the bottom of ponds, and fight with other males. During the autumn rut, when bulls are stoked by testosterone, spectacular fights erupt among bulls competing for females (cows). About eight months after mating, cows give birth to one or two offspring. Newborns weigh up to 35 pounds, and adult moose live up to 20 years in the wild.

Moose require 50 to 60 pounds of vegetation each day. They feed by wrapping thick, rubbery lips around a twig, then stripping away the leaves, bark, and buds in a single motion. The name "moose" comes from the Algonquian word *moosu*, which has been translated as "twig eater" or "he who strips off." Moose meat was a staple of native diets, and moose hides were used to make leather moccasins.

Roughly 80 percent of North America's moose population lives in Canada, but they are relatively recent arrivals. Moose crossed the Bering land bridge during the Ice Age and spread across upper North America. When wolves and grizzlies roamed Colorado, moose were relatively rare, but those predators have not been present for decades. In 1978, Colorado reintroduced 24 moose to North Park, some of which migrated into Rocky Mountain National Park. Today there are several dozen moose in the park. They are most common near Kawuneeche Valley, but some venture east of the Continental Divide.

Mountain Lion

Felis concolor

Mountain lions (also called cougars, pumas, panthers, and catamounts) are the largest predators in Rocky Mountain National Park. Males weigh over 200 pounds and measure more than eight feet from nose to tail. Females weigh up to 140 pounds and measure seven feet long. Mountain lions have the largest proportional hind legs of any feline. They can jump nearly 20 feet vertically and 40 feet horizontally, and they can run up to 50 mph. Retractable claws aid in both hunting and tree climbing. Mountain lions are found from Canada to Argentina—the most extensive range of any mammal (except humans) in the Western Hemisphere—and they are the second-largest wildcats in the Western Hemisphere after jaguars.

Mountain lions travel up to 25 miles a day in search of food, killing prey every four to eight days. Excellent night vision enables them to hunt from dusk till dawn. They are quick, efficient hunters that quietly stalk prey before pouncing. Victims often die from a lethal bite to the spinal cord. In Rocky Mountain National Park, mountain lions hunt elk, mule deer, and bighorn sheep, as well as smaller animals like rabbits, squirrels, and chipmunks.

Solitary and territorial, mountain lions require an extensive home range of up to 500 square miles. Adult mountain lions come together only to mate. Females are solely responsible for parenting, and cubs stay with mothers for roughly two years while learning survival skills. Mountain lion pups are born with spots and ringed tails, but they develop a uniform tan coloration by about 2.5 years in age. Mountain lions often live around 12 years in the wild.

Before European settlement, mountain lions inhabited much of North America. In the late 1800s and early 1900s, however, they were hunted to the brink of extinction. Following the enactment of strict hunting regulations, mountain lions have

made a steady comeback in the West, and they are starting to spread east. Reclusive by nature, they go to great lengths to avoid people, and they are rarely seen in Rocky Mountain National Park. If you do encounter a mountain lion, slowly back away while holding a steady gaze.

Coyote
Canis latrans

Coyotes roam Rocky Mountain National Park during the day, and their haunting howls echo through the mountains at night. One long, high-pitched howl calls a pack of coyotes together, and when the pack has gathered a cacophony of yips and yelps are often added to the mix. Coyotes have brownish-gray fur and long, bushy tails. Unlike dogs and wolves, coyotes run with their tails hanging down.

Coyotes currently range from Canada to Panama, but historically they were confined to the open spaces of the western U.S. and Mexico. Following the extermination of wolves in the 1800s, coyotes spread rapidly throughout North America. Intelligent, adaptable animals with a knack for scavenging, coyote populations have held steady and even increased in places despite years of being hunted, poisoned, and trapped. This is partly due to an amazing reproductive adaptation: when coyote populations decline, the remaining animals breed at younger ages and produce larger litters.

Although coyotes often forage alone, they sometimes travel in packs of six or so closely related family members. Their diet, which is 90 percent animals, consists mostly of rodents and small mammals. But coyotes eat just about anything, including birds, snakes, insects, carrion, and trash. Working in packs, coyotes hunt larger animals such as deer and bighorn sheep. While pursuing prey, they can reach top speeds of over 40 mph and jump up to 13 feet horizontally.

Coyotes are strictly monogamous. They mate in winter, and mothers give birth to five to seven pups in spring. Newborn coyote are hairless and sightless, and they don't leave the den until eight to ten weeks of age. Young coyotes are extremely vulnerable. Up to two-thirds do not survive to adulthood, but those that survive can live 10 years or longer in the wild. Adult coyotes measure up to four feet long and weigh up to 50 pounds.

Coyotes often play a central role in the legends and myths of native tribes. Among a small cast of human and animal characters, Coyote is portrayed as a scheming trickster that scrapes by on cunning and charm. The word "coyote" is derived from the Aztec word *cóyotl*. Coyote's Latin name, *Canis latrans*, means "barking dog," a reference to its famous vocalizations.

Yellow-Bellied Marmot
Marmota flaviventris

These roly-poly rodents are western cousins of groundhogs and woodchucks. In Rocky Mountain National Park they are generally found above treeline. Marmots live in colonies of 10 to 20 animals, and they live in elaborate burrows underground. During the short summer season, marmots are aggressive food opportunists, eating as much as possible and packing on thick layers of fat to survive the harsh winter ahead. Their diet includes leaves, grasses, berries, flowers, insects, and bird eggs. By autumn, some marmots can weigh 12 pounds or more. During hibernation, their body temperature drops from 97°F to 40°F, their heartbeat drops to four beats per minute, and they breathe once every six minutes. After emerging from their roughly 200-day hibernation, male marmots dig new dens under rock piles and gather a harem of up to four females. Female marmots have litters of three to five pups, but only about half survive their first year. Adult marmots can live up to 15 years in the wild.

American Marten
Martes americana

American martens, also called pine martens, are tree-dwelling predators that belong to the weasel family. Their range extends across much of Alaska, Canada, and mountain regions in the lower 48 states. Lodgepole pines and Douglas-fir are among their favorite trees. Mostly nocturnal, martens prey on small animals such as chickarees, pikas, and voles. Opportunistic omnivores, martens also eat insects, birds, fish, fruits, and nuts. Marten predators include mountain lions, coyotes, and raptors. Incredibly agile, martens climb down trees head first. They can also swim underwater and travel across deep snow. Martens are active all winter and do not hibernate. Large males measure over two feet long from their pointed snout to the tip of their bushy tail. Adult martens live largely solitary lives until breeding season in summer. Fertilized eggs do not implant until winter, and females give birth to a litter of two to three kits. Martens often live a dozen or more years in the wild.

American Pika
Ochotona princeps

Found among the parks highest elevations, these adorable animals spend short summers furiously gathering plants in preparation for winter. Unlike other alpine mammals, pikas don't hibernate. They simply hunker in their dens for up to 10 months, munching on stored "hay piles." Insulated by thick layers of snow, pika dens are cozy, quiet places. They are located in rock fields and talus that offer protected nooks. Pikas don't burrow underground, but they will dig snow tunnels in winter to search for extra food. Two different pika subspecies, northern and southern, meet in Rocky Mountain National Park. Although pikas look like rodents, they are actually the smallest members of the rabbit family. Large, round ears help them communicate. Males use a long whistling sound to defend territory, and a loud "eeep" warns neighbors of predators such as hawks, eagles, martens, and weasels. Female pikas have two litters each summer. After four months, young pikas are largely independent. Adults measure seven inches long, weigh six ounces, and live up to seven years. Pikas are sensitive to temperatures above 75°F, which makes them vulnerable to global warming.

Snowshoe Hare
Lepus americanus

Snowshoe hares are masters of disguise. In summer they sport a grayish brown coat that helps them blend in with grasses and shrubs. As winter approaches, their coat turns white, providing excellent camouflage in snow. Snowshoe hare predators include foxes, coyotes, owls, and hawks. When a hare senses a predator, it freezes to avoid detection. If necessary, it can flee at speeds up to 30 mph, hopping 12 feet in a single bound and making sharp zigzags. Snowshoe hares often spend their days sleeping in hidden locations, becoming active only at night or in the low light of dawn or dusk. They mate and give birth year-round. Females produce up to eight young per litter, up to four times per year. Young hares can run within hours of birth. Snowshoe hare populations are cyclical, becoming plentiful every 10 years or so, then plummeting dramatically. During population booms, some areas contain up to 10,000 snowshoe hares per square mile.

Beaver
Castor canadensis

Weighing 40 pounds or more, beavers are the largest rodents in North America. They use large incisors to topple trees and drag them to streams to build dams. The resulting wetlands create prime habitat for beavers and boost the area's overall biodiversity. Beavers construct dams with logs, sticks, and rocks cemented with mud. They build a living space, called a lodge, by heaping together a separate pile of debris, then gnawing out a roomy chamber from below. Beavers are excellent swimmers that can remain submerged up to 15 minutes. Large, webbed hind feet aid in swimming, and they use long, flat tails as rudders while towing trees and branches in water. Native tribes considered roasted beaver tail a delicacy, and European settlers paid high prices for beaver pelts. By the 1800s, however, beaver populations were in serious decline. They recovered following the collapse of the beaver trade, but in the 1940s beaver populations crashed in Rocky Mountain National Park. This was largely due to booming elk herds, which overgrazed tall willows on which beavers depend for food and shelter. Until willows recover, beavers will remain relatively rare in the park.

North American River Otter
Lontra canadensis

Found in rivers and lakes, these playful members of the weasel family are well adapted to acquatic environments. Powerful tails and webbed feet propel them through water, and they can stay submerged for eight minutes. Thick, water-repellent fur keeps them warm year-round. When otters dive they seal their ears and nostrils. A third eyelid helps them see underwater, and long whiskers detect prey in cloudy water. Incredibly agile, otters twist, roll, and make lightning-fast turns to catch fish, frogs, and salamanders. Large otters weigh over 30 pounds and measure over three feet long, one-third of which is the tail. River otters live in burrows near rivers and lakes. They are equally at home on land, where they enjoy sliding on snow in winter. In Rocky Mountain National Park, river otters live in and around the Colorado River in Kawuneeche Valley.

Greenback Cutthroat Trout
Oncorhynchus clarkii stomias

One of seven native fish in the park, greenback cutthroat trout live in lakes and streams east of the Continental Divide. Cutthroat trout are named for a blood-red streak under their jaw. Habitat loss and non-native trout species decimated populations in the late 1800s, and greenbacks were declared extinct in 1937. Then, in the 1950s, isolated populations were rediscovered. Restoration programs have significantly boosted populations over the past several decades. In 1996 greenback cutthroat trout became the official state fish of Colorado.

Western Garter Snake
Thamnophis elegans

The only snake in Rocky Mountain National Park lives in the park's lower elevations. Western garter snakes measure about three feet long, and they are the only garter snakes in the world that constrict their prey. Although they have a mildly poisonous saliva, they are harmless to humans. Western garter snakes feed on both terrestrial and aquatic animals. Instead of laying eggs, females give birth to live snakes.

Tiger Salamander
Ambystoma tigrinum

Measuring one foot or longer and weighing up to two pounds, tiger salamanders are the world's largest land salamanders. They spend most of their lives in underground burrows, emerging at night to prey on worms, frogs, insects, and mice. Salamanders often live near ponds, where females lay up to 100 eggs. Adults can live 14 years or more. Tiger salamanders range across much of the U.S., southern Canada, and eastern Mexico.

HISTORY

EVIDENCE OF HUMAN activity in Colorado dates back roughly 13,000 years. In the depths of the Ice Age, when enormous glaciers trapped much of earth's water, sea levels dropped, and Siberian hunters crossed the Bering land bridge, fanning out across North America. The continental ice sheets covering much of Canada and the northern U.S. did not extend into Colorado, but smaller glaciers flowed down from the Rockies. By the time Paleo-Indians arrived, global temperatures were rising and glaciers were in retreat.

Paleo-Indians encountered a rugged landscape filled with enormous creatures. Giant ground sloths, seven-foot-long beavers, saber-tooth tigers, dire wolves, short-faced bears, camels, and eight-foot-tall bison roamed the landscape. Perhaps most impressive was the woolly mammoth, a shaggy, eight-ton elephant-like creature with 10-foot tusks. To hunt these massive animals, Paleo-Indians crafted five-inch-long stone projectile points, called Clovis points, that attached to wooden spears. Spear-throwers called atlatls magnified the weapon's power and range. Clovis points are famous for their center groove, called a flute, but its exact purpose is unknown and its design is unique to the Americas.

Most large Ice Age animals went extinct around 11,000 years ago. Whether Paleo-Indians hunted them to extinction is a matter of debate. With the largest animals gone, hunters crafted smaller projectile points, called Folsom points, to hunt the giant bison that remained. Men fashioned Folsom points out of chert and jasper, but the best points were made of obsidian, a sharp volcanic glass often traded over long distances. Folsom point flutes extend nearly the entire length of the point, a design that required great technical skill. Archaeologists consider Folsom points among the finest stone tools ever made.

Wooden tools and animal skin clothes disintegrate over time, but projectile points and stone tools can last thousands of years. The world's most extensive Folsom culture archaeological site, the Lindenmeier Site, is located 40 miles northeast of Rocky Mountain National Park. In addition to utilitarian objects like Folsom points, stone knives, and bone needles, the site contains decorative items and gaming pieces, suggesting a complex social life. Over 50,000 artifacts have been discovered at Lindenmeier, including stone manos to grind seeds and roots, which women likely harvested nearby.

Around 7,000 years ago, giant bison also became extinct, and hunters turned to smaller bison, deer, and bighorn sheep. They also hunted rabbits, squirrels, mice, birds, snakes, and lizards. Women harvested a wide variety of wild plants, further expanding the tribe's diet. This new culture, the Archaic Indians, lived in small, nomadic bands that followed migrating animals and ripening plants. Portable animal hide tents, carried by dogs from camp to camp, provided shelter when natural protection like caves or rock overhangs were unavailable.

Spring, summer, and fall were times of abundance. In winter, Archaic Indians survived off preserved foods including pemmican (jerky), a dried mixture of pulverized meat, berries, and fat. Lacking pottery, women cooked stews in water-proof baskets or animal stomachs, dropping fire-heated rocks into the liquid until it boiled. Rabbit-fur clothing and blankets provided warmth.

Colorado's Front Range, which stretches roughly 300 miles along the east slope of the Rockies, was particularly attractive to humans. Dozens of rivers tumble down the mountains, and lingering snowbanks keep the area well-watered year-round—a sharp contrast to the arid eastern plains. Rising nearly 10,000 feet above shortgrass prairie, the Front Range compresses a wide range of ecological zones into a relatively small area, offering a remarkable natural bounty.

Around 2,000 years ago, agriculture and pottery spread to the Front Range from eastern tribes. Pottery allowed women to boil water directly over an open fire, and clay storage vessels offered better protection from pests than baskets. Another technological breakthrough was the bow and arrow. Powerful, accurate, and boasting a far longer range than spears, the new weapon allowed hunters to sneak up on prey and silently release arrows with the flick of a finger.

In Rocky Mountain National Park, tribes climbed above treeline to hunt elk and bighorn sheep, which graze the vast expanses of alpine tundra. But the open spaces offer almost no cover, so hunters employed a clever strategy. They built extensive rock walls, designed in conjunction with natural barriers and prevailing winds, to funnel animals toward a kill zone where downwind hunters hid in blinds. Over 50 "game drives," some over a half-mile long, exist in and around Rocky Mountain National Park—more than anywhere else in Colorado.

High-altitude game drives were part of a seasonal "grand circuit" that looped over 200 miles across the Continental Divide. Tribes spent winter in the warmer eastern foothills, which offered easy access to buffalo roaming the plains. After gathering Lyons sandstone—used to grind seeds and sharpen stones—small bands headed north in spring, crossed the Continental Divide at snow-free passes, and spent early summer in lush North Park enjoying abundant plants and game.

In midsummer, small bands converged in Middle Park and the Kawuneeche Valley, then moved in large groups to seasonal hunting camps in Rocky Mountain National Park. Forest Canyon Pass and Beaver Meadows, located on opposite ends of the Ute Trail, were two of the park's most important camps. From Forest Canyon Pass, hunters enjoyed easy access to alpine tundra along both Mt. Ida and Trail Ridge. Other camps were located below Flattop Mountain, which con-

tains one of the most extensive game drive systems in Colorado. It has nine game drives, 14 stone walls, and 90 blinds. Dozens of people may have participated in communal hunts. After harvesting game, hunters butchered the carcasses and carried them back to camp. At the end of alpine tundra hunting season, large groups disbanded and descended to the foothills to spend winter.

Roughly 800 years ago, a new tribe, the Utes, arrived from the Great Basin Desert to the west. Fierce and resourceful, Utes soon dominated Colorado's mountains. After acquiring horses, they further expanded their territory across the eastern plains. Although horses evolved in North America, they abandoned the continent for Asia during the Ice Age—only to be reintroduced by the Spanish in the 1500s. Tribes that acquired horses, whether through barter or theft, gained a huge strategic advantage. Great Plains tribes became some of the most formidable horse riders the world has ever known, thundering across vast distances, slaughtering bison with ease, and raiding enemy tribes.

Eventually most Colorado tribes acquired horses, including the Arapahoes, who arrived in the early 1800s. The Arapahoes spent much of the year hunting bison on the plains, but they made regular excursions into the Front Range, particularly the region around Rocky Mountain National Park. The mountains offered bountiful game, edible plants, and an endless supply of wood, which was in short supply on the treeless plains. The mountains also brought the Arapahoes into contact with the Utes, and the tribes soon became enemies.

Life was changing fast in Colorado. Horses and guns, acquired through vast trading networks, unleashed explosive new forms of power that altered native lifestyles and led to a population surge. But even greater changes lurked on the eastern horizon, where a new nation was moving west.

UTE

Utes are the mountain tribe of Colorado, but they originally hailed from the western deserts, arriving roughly 800 years ago. The word *Ute* (from which Utah is derived) means "Land of the Sun." They call themselves *Nuche*, "The People," and their origin story tells of the creator Sinawaf placing sticks in a bag, which Coyote, the trickster, opened while Sinawaf was away. People speaking different languages jumped out, scattering in all directions and creating chaos. Only the Utes remained in the bag, and when Sinawaf returned he declared "they will be very brave and able to defeat the rest."

The Utes were skilled warriors feared by neighboring tribes. Highly nomadic, they roamed the Rockies seasonally in search of game and plants. After acquiring horses in the 1600s, their range extended across the eastern plains. But when their neighbors, the Comanches, acquired guns from French traders they forced the Utes back into the mountains, where they largely remained.

Among the most important Ute ceremonies is *mama-kwa-nhhap*, the Bear Dance, held in spring after the first thunder. The multi-day ceremony gives thanks to Ta-vwoats (Great Spirit) for surviving the harsh winter and renewing life, symbolized by the Bear emerging from hibernation. Men and women line up on opposite sides, and women walk forward to choose dance partners with the wave of a shawl. The dance is presided over by Cat Man, and singers use wooden rasps to imitate the growl of the Bear. On the final day of the Bear Dance, men and women pair up and dance rapidly, the music continuing until someone falls down.

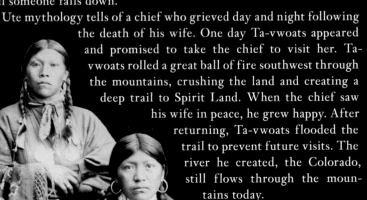

Ute mythology tells of a chief who grieved day and night following the death of his wife. One day Ta-vwoats appeared and promised to take the chief to visit her. Ta-vwoats rolled a great ball of fire southwest through the mountains, crushing the land and creating a deep trail to Spirit Land. When the chief saw his wife in peace, he grew happy. After returning, Ta-vwoats flooded the trail to prevent future visits. The river he created, the Colorado, still flows through the mountains today.

ARAPAHO

The Arapahoes arrived in Colorado after an extended migration across the Great Plains. Originally from Minnesota, they were pushed west in the 1700s by neighboring tribes who acquired European guns. For decades the Arapahoes roamed the plains on foot. After acquiring horses they became skilled bison hunters, and by the early 1800s they lived along northern Colorado's Front Range. They refer to themselves as *Inunaina*, "Our People."

Gifted traders, the Arapahoes formed alliances with several neighboring tribes, most notably the Cheyenne, who called them "Cloud People." Their enemies, including the Utes, called them "Dog Eaters" because they sometimes ate dogs. The Arapahoes believe *Houu*, "Man Above," created the Rocky Mountains to separate them from the Utes, with whom they often fought. The Arapahoes generally won battles on the Plains, while the Utes held the upper hand in the mountains.

The Arapahoes' most important ceremony is the Sun Dance—a multi-day event often held in spring. As the tribe feasted, male dancers fasted until the final night, then pierced their chest muscles with skewers made of sticks or eagle claws. The skewers were tethered to the top of a tall pole, and the men danced in a frenzy, straining until their flesh broke and they collapsed in pain. Dancers were sometimes hoisted high above ground until gravity broke their flesh. Most Plains tribes practice a version of the Sun Dance, as do the Utes (who avoid the self-mutilation).

During the Sun Dance, offerings are made to *Seicha*, "Flat Pipe," the Arapahoes' most sacred object. The long pipe is considered a spirit being that was present when all was water, and a turtle dove to the bottom to gather mud, from which Flat Pipe created the earth. Flat Pipe is smoked only at night, and its full creation myth takes three nights to tell.

Vision quests play an important role in Arapaho spiritual life. One of the most famous vision quest sites is Old Man Mountain in Estes Park. Vision seekers hauled large river boulders to the peak, then fasted alone for several days and nights, awaiting visions of a spirit animal to guide them in future endeavors.

Clothing

Native women used animal hides to make soft, durable clothing. Ute women, in particular, were renowned for their ability to prepare beautiful, luxuriant buckskin. They crafted shirts, dresses, and leggings from the soft hides of deer and elk. Thick bison hides made durable moccasin soles, while the soft hide of bison calves was used for undergarments and baby swaddles. Hides with animal fur provided extra warmth for mittens and hats. Buffalo hides harvested in winter, when the fur is thickest, were prized for warm robes. Women traditionally decorated clothes with porcupine quills, elk teeth, and bone beads. Following the arrival of European traders, manufactured beads became increasingly popular.

Tipis

Portable, sturdy, waterproof, and easily erected, tipis are remarkable feats of engineering used as shelter by Plains tribes. Wooden poles are lashed together at one end, then raised with a twist to interlock the poles, forming a conical frame that is covered with stitched buffalo hides. The hides are then latched shut with wooden pegs along a vertical seam. Adjustable twin flaps at the top control ventilation, keeping tipis warm in winter and cool in summer. The tipi entrance faces east to greet the rising sun and offer protection against prevailing western winds. A tipi's slightly tilted conical shape provides structural support against strong winds, with the added benefit of creating more headroom in the back. Before Plains tribes acquired horses, dogs carried small tipis on travois—a trailer made of poles that drag on the ground. Horses could carry significantly more weight, so tipis grew much larger, increasing from five feet to 15 feet in height. A central fire is used for both warmth and cooking. Prior to the arrival of white settlers, tipis glowed like lanterns across the Great Plains at night.

Headdress

Headdresses, sometimes called war bonnets, are traditionally worn by male leaders of Colorado tribes. They are often decorated with feathers from eagles (the most powerful and respected birds), which must be earned through acts of bravery. Often this was done by counting coup, the daring act of touching an enemy in battle, which was considered more heroic than killing. Feathers can also be earned through political success, diplomatic victories, or acts that strengthen the tribe.

Cradleboards

Mothers carried babies in cradleboards for the first year or two of their lives. The rigid wooden frame and basketry hood provided protection, while a snug leather pouch lined with fur and eagle down kept babies warm. A light covering could be pulled across the hood to provide shade and deter insects while napping. Grasses and soft bark served as diapers. Women often carried cradleboards on their backs, but they could also be hung from branches or tipi poles. When traveling, cradleboards could be attached to the side of a horse or across a travois. Young girls sometimes carried puppies in small craddleboards in preparation for motherhood.

Sun Dance & Bear Dance

Ute depiction of the Sun Dance and Bear Dance (right). Bear Dance wooden rasp used as a "growl" stick (below)

EXPLORERS & MOUNTAIN MEN

The first Europeans to enter Colorado were Spanish colonists, who set forth from Santa Fe, New Mexico, in the early 1600s. After failing to find gold, Spain largely ignored its rugged northern territory. France later gained control of "Louisiana," which extended to the eastern Rocky Mountains, and by the late 1700s French mountain men were trickling into Colorado.

The men came in search of beaver pelts, which fetched high prices for their use in felt hats. Mountain men were notoriously rugged, and they often set out on year-long expeditions loaded with knives, kettles, cloth, beads, and other manufactured goods to trade with local tribes. Many mountain men married native women and adopted largely native lifestyles, speaking a strange pastiche of French, Spanish, English, and Indian words. For several decades these buckskin-clad master woodsmen were the only whites who visited Colorado.

In 1803, the United States purchased Louisiana from France for $15 million. Three years later, a government expedition led by Zebulon Pike reached the eastern slope of the Rocky Mountains. One peak towered above all others, and in November Pike attempted—and failed—to climb the 14,115-foot mountain. Pike assumed it was the highest peak in the Rockies. It wasn't, but Pikes Peak, as the mountain came to be called, would eventually become famous nonetheless.

As word of Colorado's natural bounty spread, more mountain men arrived. In 1819, the U.S. government organized a group of scientists, engineers, and artists to investigate the region's economic potential. The following year Major Stephen Long led the 22-man Yellowstone Expedition across present-day Nebraska. Long called the Great Plains "the great American Desert" and determined it was "almost wholly unfit for cultivation." As the expedition neared the Rockies, the men saw a summit even taller than Pikes Peak. Although Long only viewed the mountain from a distance, he became the first white man to formally record its existence, and today Longs Peak is the highest summit in Rocky Mountain National Park.

Trappers scoured the mountains around Longs Peak in the 1820s, and trading posts opened along the nearby South Platte River. Both trappers and natives brought beaver pelts and bison hides to trade for manufactured goods. The Arapahoes called white people *niatha*, "spider," for the clever and skillful items they produced.

But European trade networks also brought deadly diseases like smallpox, which killed nearly half of the Plains Indians in the 1830s. This trag-

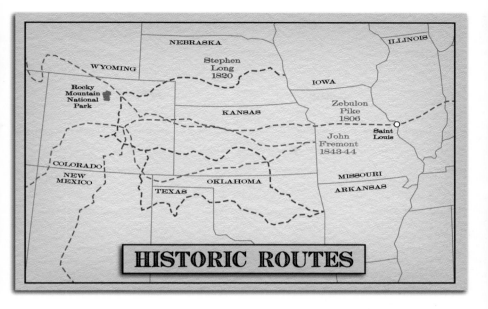

HISTORIC ROUTES

edy was followed by the collapse of the beaver pelt industry after cheap Chinese silk flooded the hat-making market. By the 1840s, many trading posts had closed.

The mountain man era was drawing to a close, but explorers continued to investigate the region's possibilities. In 1843, Rufus B. Sage visited present-day Estes Park and marveled at the scenery. "A lake," he wrote, "occupies the center of a basinlike valley, bounded in every direction by verdant hills, that smile upon the bright gem embosomed among them. ... What a charming retreat for some one of the world-hating *literati*! He might here hold daily converse with himself, Nature, and his God, far removed from the annoyance of man."

The next year famed explorer John Fremont searched for a pass through the Rockies, at one point traveling just west of present-day Rocky Mountain National Park. The pass never materialized, and Fremont, a keen observer of the West, lamented that both Indians and bison "are visibly diminishing."

In 1848, following the Mexican-American War, the U.S. acquired over half a million square miles stretching from the Rocky Mountains to the Pacific Ocean. The timing was perfect. Prospectors discovered gold in California that same year, and tens of thousands of people set out across the Great Plains. Despite the frenzy of wagon trains, northern Colorado remained relatively isolated. Gold seekers on the California-Oregon Trail passed through Wyoming to the north. Those following the Santa Fe Trail passed through southern Colorado. In between lay the Rocky Mountains—a formidable barrier to travel.

But the same shiny metal that drew thousands to California also lay deep in the Rockies. And when prospectors discovered it, the history of Colorado would forever change.

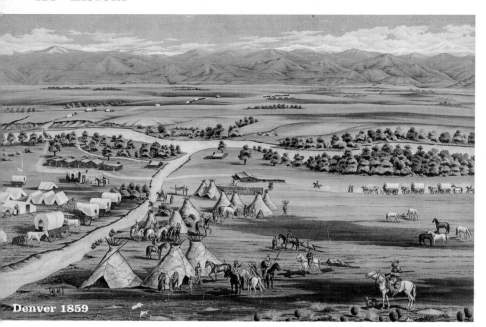

Denver 1859

THE COLORADO GOLD RUSH

The 1850s were boom years in America. As California gold flooded the market, the economy thrived, but easy riches triggered a speculative bubble. That bubble burst in 1857, when a banking crisis sank the country into depression. Two years later gold was discovered in the Rockies, and thousands of people seeking better lives flooded into Colorado. Within a decade, the Colorado Gold Rush drew twice as many fortune seekers across the Great Plains as the California Gold Rush.

Rumors of gold had been circulating for years, mostly among semi-reputable mountain men. One story involved Arapahoes fashioning golden bullets out of the soft, shiny metal. But ever since the Spanish abandoned their search centuries earlier, tales of gold were largely dismissed as drunken ramblings.

By the 1850s, however, credible new rumors were flourishing. In 1858, over 150 gold hunters descended on the Front Range. They found traces of gold, but the quantities were so pitiful that most people gave up. Then, on July 6, William Russell led a handful of prospectors along Little Dry Creek, just south of present-day Denver, and discovered a streambed speckled with gold.

Russell's find was small but promising. Word quickly spread, and a trader named John Cantrell came by for a look. Cantrell gathered some gold, headed to Kansas City, and theatrically revealed the glittering metal to a crowd of dazzled onlookers. "THE NEW ELDORADO!!!" blared local newspapers, "The Pike's Mines!!!" News of Rocky Mountain gold, just 600 miles west of Kansas City, radiated across America, and soon the rush was on. Over 100,000 people headed to newly founded Denver City the following year. Big strikes confirmed the hype was real. Pikes Peak, visible far across the eastern plains, became a beacon for "Fifty-Niners" heading west, and "Pike's Peak or Bust" decorated covered wagons.

The flood of gold and people brought wealth to Colorado, but it proved disastrous for local tribes. Tensions between whites and Indians had been festering for years. Unlike mountain men, who often married into local tribes, the new arrivals kept their distance, and skirmishes grew increasingly common.

Plains tribes had also become almost entirely dependent on bison, which they hunted with ruthless precision on horseback. Bison herds once covered 300 square miles during mating congregations, but the herds were shrinking, and bison no longer roamed the Front Range when prospectors arrived. Each spring the Arapahoes and Cheyennes rode east, where large bison herds remained, then returned to the Front Range to spend winter. When they returned in 1858, a bustling white settlement lay along Cherry Creek and the South Platte River.

The Arapaho chief Niwot, "Left Hand," grasped the powerful forces at play, and he counseled friendly relations with whites. Young warriors, led by a man named Heap of Whips, thirsted for confrontation. The same dynamic played out among the Cheyennes, and fierce divisions tore through both tribes.

The situation grew increasingly desperate. Livestock that powered western wagon trains further depleted the Great Plains, which Plains tribes had been depleting for decades. Pandemics, intertribal wars, collapsing natural resources, and reduced demand for bison hides took a devastating toll on Colorado tribes. Within a few years, many were on the brink of starvation.

In 1861, Congress created Colorado Territory (previously part of Kansas and Nebraska Territory), and politicians pressured tribes to relocate to reservations and adopt agrarian lives. Many horse warriors had no interest in performing women's work, but pacifist factions gave it a try. The results were dismal, in large part because promised supplies never materialized. Meanwhile, scattered attacks by militant factions inflamed white settlers, who demanded retaliation.

In 1864, a ragtag militia headed southeast from Denver to Sand Creek, where dozens of largely pacifist Arapaho and Cheyenne families were struggling to make it through winter. As the militia thundered toward them, Cheyenne leader Black Kettle held an American flag high and promised his people the troops would not harm them. The troops opened fire, slaughtering over 200 people, mostly women, children, and the elderly. Chief Niwot was among the dead.

The Sand Creek Massacre plunged Plains tribes into open revolt, followed by a series of ineffective peace treaties. The Utes, meanwhile, remained relatively sheltered in the mountains. But as miners pushed deep into Colorado's rich mineral belt, they forced the Utes to cede their once-vast territory for a small reservation in southwest Colorado. It was more than the Arapahoes received. As more settlers arrived, they pushed the Arapahoes out of Colorado entirely, forcing them onto reservations in Wyoming and Oklahoma.

Lulu City

The Colorado Gold Rush produced over one million ounces of gold in its first five years, but by the late 1860s production had stagnated. Then, in 1879, prospectors discovered silver in Leadville, kicking off the Colorado Silver Boom. Mining towns flourished throughout the Colorado Mineral Belt, which stretches over 200 miles from Boulder to Durango.

In June 1879, Joe Shipler headed into the mountains west of Fort Collins and discovered silver near the headwaters of the Colorado River in present-day Rocky Mountain National Park. The next year William Baker and Benjamin Burnett founded Lulu City, named for Burnett's eldest daughter. "New discoveries are being found every day," boasted *The Colorado Miner*. "Blasts can be heard at any hour of the day from mines in hearing of Lulu City." Eager miners poured into the remote valley, and by 1882 Lulu City boasted 500 residents and 40 buildings. The Godsmark and Parker Hotel boasted "fine linen, lovely silverware and sparkling glasses." A red-light district north of town consisted of two cozy cabins. "There is no doubt of a grand future for the camp," declared the *Rocky Mountain News*.

It was all an illusion. By the end of 1882, the region produced just $10,000 worth of precious metals—the least of any mining county in Colorado. Within a year Lulu City was abandoned. Only Joe Shipler remained, working his North Star Mine for the next 30 years, until eventually even he gave up. Today Lulu City is the ultimate ghost town. Not even the buildings remain.

ESTES PARK

The Colorado Gold Rush brought tens of thousands of settlers to Colorado, not all of whom found riches in gold. Many took to farming and ranching thanks to the 1862 Homestead Act, which allowed settlers to claim 160 acres if they cultivated the land, built a structure, and paid a small fee.

Among the new arrivals was Joel Estes, a Missouri farmer who went to California during the Gold Rush, came back with a small fortune, then headed to Colorado in 1859 to look for more gold. While exploring the mountains near Longs Peak, Estes stumbled upon a hidden valley centered around a beautiful lake. "No words," his son Milton later wrote, "can describe our surprise, wonder and joy at beholding such an unexpected sight."

Estes moved his family to the valley in 1863 to graze cattle and homestead the land. "We were monarchs of all we surveyed," Milton recalled. "We had a little world all to ourselves." Estes and his son hunted elk, deer, and bighorn sheep, selling the meat and hides in Denver for a tidy profit.

The next year William Byers, editor of the *Rocky Mountain News*, visited Estes and wrote a glowing report about the "sylvan paradise," which he dubbed Estes Park. "The landscape struck us at first sight as one of the most lovely we ever beheld," Byers gushed. "Eventually this park will become a favorite pleasure resort." Estes abandoned the valley in 1866 because of the cold, lonely winters, but the name Estes Park stuck.

Legend has it that Joel Estes traded his namesake valley for a yoke of oxen. By the late 1860s, a Welshman named Griffith Evans settled on Estes' former property. Evans moved to Colorado in 1863, but soon after arriving he lost his life's savings in a business swindle. It was late fall when he moved his wife and three children to Estes Park. The family moved into Estes' abandoned cabin, survived winter despite meager resources, and adopted a challenging but satisfying life.

As word of the beautiful valley spread, a handful of travelers stopped by to see it firsthand. Evans, sensing a new business opportunity, built guest cabins on his property. He decorated his rustic lodge with antlers and Indian weapons. Entertainment consisted of Welsh songs and "out-of-date dances."

In 1873, an unusual visitor passed through: Windham Thomas Wyndham-Quin, fourth Earl of Dunraven and Mount-Earl Ireland. The Irish nobleman had spent the past few months hunting big game in the West, traveling with an extended entourage. While exploring Colorado, Dunraven heard about fabulous hunting in Estes Park, so he came by for a look.

Dunraven was so taken with Estes Park—"great, glorious, heavily timbered valleys and cañons ... a paradise for the hunter and trapper"—that he returned the following year, and the year after that. Eventually he decided to acquire the entire valley. Dunraven purchased Evans' property and, with the help of Denver lawyers, convinced 35 men to homestead 160 acres each in Estes Park, then sell him their titled property. Despite this quasi-legal maneuver, Dunraven acquired roughly 6,000 acres.

The *Denver Tribune* called Dunraven's actions "one of the most villainous land steals ever perpetrated in Colorado." Within a few years courts forced him to relinquish nearly half of his holdings. Undeterred, Dunraven spent nearly $300,000 developing the vast acreage that remained. According to the *Denver Post,* his personal lodge was "one of the finest summer homes in Colorado." Dunraven also built a three-story hotel—its stunning hilltop location personally selected by famous landscape painter Albert Bierstadt (p.120)—where he entertained visiting English nobility.

EARL OF DUNRAVEN

As Dunraven developed Estes Park, half a dozen settlers took up residence in the surrounding wilderness. One was Illinois native Abner Sprague, who in 1875 claimed 160 acres in Moraine Park (then called Willow Park) and later opened a tourist lodge. Another was the Rev. Elkanah Lamb, who claimed property near the eastern base of Longs Peak in 1875. Lamb also opened a lodge and guided climbers up Longs Peak for $5 a trip. The age of tourism had officially begun. By the end of the decade Dunraven declared, "The marks of carriage wheels are more plentiful than elk signs."

ISABELLA BIRD & ROCKY MOUNTAIN JIM

In 1873, English traveler Isabella Bird (right) visited Estes Park and stayed at Griffith Evans' lodge. While exploring the valley—"Nothing that I have seen in Colorado compares with Estes Park"—she met James Nugent, better known as Rocky Mountain Jim. He was a colorful recluse with a mixed reputation. "Desperado was written in large letters all over him," Bird wrote. Despite losing one eye to a grizzly, Jim "must have been strikingly handsome," and he charmed Bird with his chivalrous manners.

ISABELLA BIRD

Bird enlisted Jim to guide her to the top of Longs Peak, an endeavor that filled her with "extreme terror." She wanted to quit near the summit, but "Jim dragged me up, like a bale of goods, by sheer force of muscle." Bird developed a tender affection for Jim, but she rejected his advances. He was a "man any woman could love, but no sane woman would marry." After urging Jim to give up whisky, "which at present is his ruin," Bird left Estes Park.

The next year Jim grew angry with Griffith Evans. Some said Jim was upset Evans sold his land to the Earl of Dunraven, who also wanted Jim's land near the entrance to Estes Park. Others claimed Jim developed an interest in Evans' 17-year-old daughter, who was seen with William Haigh, a young Englishmen visiting Dunraven. Whatever the cause, tensions quickly escalated.

On June 19, Rocky Mountain Jim approached Griffith Evans' ranch. Evans claimed Jim threatened to kill him. As Jim described it, Evans "approached me with a double-barreled shot gun ... and shot me ... through the head." Miraculously Jim survived, even though, as Dunraven put it, "he had one bullet in his skull and his brains were oozing out." Jim traveled to Fort Collins for medical attention, and police charged Evans with assault with a deadly weapon with intent to kill.

While recovering, Jim wrote an impassioned letter to the local newspaper, pleading his innocence and claiming Haigh had ordered his execution. The media sided with Haigh, "a traveling English gentleman of wealth and leisure. ... We sincerely trust his annoyances may not disgust him with our territory." A judge found Evans not guilty, writing "The only blame which can be attached to Mr. Evans is that he did not give Jim the deserved dose long ago."

Rocky Mountain Jim died of the gunshot wound on September 7, 1874. After hearing the news, Isabella Bird never visited Colorado again. She continued roaming the world, and in 1890 she became the first female member of Britain's Royal Geographic Society. Her Colorado adventures, including Jim's tragic backstory, are chronicled in her memoir *A Lady's Life in the Rocky Mountains*.

Albert Bierstadt

In 1875, artist Albert Bierstadt visited Estes Park at the invitation of the Earl of Dunraven. Bierstadt was one of the world's most famous landscape painters, and his epic portrayals of the West drew blockbuster crowds in Eastern cities, offering a rare glimpse of America's exotic hinterlands. A master of self-promotion, Bierstadt displayed his enormous paintings as if they were performances, charging admission, unveiling them from behind velvet curtains, lighting them dramatically, and recommending people view them through binoculars to heighten the visual effect. Dunraven commissioned Bierstadt to paint Estes Park and Longs Peak for $15,000, then sent the finished work to Dunraven Castle in Wales. Bierstadt Lake and Bierstadt Moraine were named after the famous artist, and today his 40-square-foot painting, *Estes Park, Longs Peak*, is at the Denver Art Museum.

SCENIC GOLD

Colorado gained statehood in 1876—the 100th anniversary of the United States. A century, earlier the Centennial State was a rugged wilderness dominated by some of the most remarkable tribes in North America. Now the tribes were largely gone, and whites had settled the Front Range. The railroad arrived in Denver in 1870, and within a decade the city boasted a population of 35,000.

In 1884, the railroad reached the small town of Lyons, from which it was just a 30-mile stage ride to Estes Park. Mountain climber Frederick Chapin followed this route in 1886, and over the next few years he climbed some of the highest peaks in present-day Rocky Mountain National Park. His 1889 guidebook, *Mountaineering in Colorado: The Peaks About Estes Park*, brought considerable attention to the region. By the 1890s, Longs Peak, first climbed in 1868 by John Wesley Powell (p.199), had become a popular destination, attracting dozens of climbers each year. "Colorado will soon be recognized as our Switzerland," predicted Bayard Taylor in his travel memoir *Colorado: A Summer Trip*.

Outdoor enthusiasts weren't the only ones exploring the mountains. In 1890, prospectors discovered gold at Cripple Creek, just southwest of Pikes Peak, kicking off yet another Colorado gold rush. A new generation of prospectors scoured the Front Range, staking over 100 claims near Longs Peak. The *Rocky Mountain News*—which never missed a chance to exploit golden dreams—reported that old-timers believed the region "will turn out to be another Cripple Creek."

Miners flocked to Longs Peak, infuriating settlers who had moved there for the region's scenic beauty. Among the most upset was Enos Mills, a young naturalist and mountain-climbing guide. "What a terrible plague is gold fever!" Mills wrote. "There are thousands of claims, and like lottery tickets, most of them are not only worthless but expensive. The piles of worthless rock dug out of valueless claims are but monuments of wasted work; while the stakes marking their boundaries are standing like headstones above buried hope."

While Longs Peak miners dug profitless holes, settlers in Estes Park discovered a nearly unlimited source of wealth: tourists. Each year brought more and more visitors, and settlers jumped at the chance to supplement their incomes. Ranchers became resort operators and shops opened "downtown" along the confluence of Fall River and Big Thompson River.

In 1905, the Earl of Dunraven sold his estate for a reported $100,000. The buyer was Freelan O. Stanley, the multimillionaire inventor of the Stanley Steamer automobile. Stanley, who suffered from tuberculosis, came to Estes Park on doctor's orders and experienced a rapid improvement in health. The wealthy auto tycoon built a sprawling new hotel, The Stanley, which opened in 1909 and became the luxury centerpiece of Estes Park. Stanley also financed the construction of a new road between Lyons and Estes Park, and Stanley Steamers delivered visiting guests in style.

ROCKY MOUNTAIN NATIONAL PARK

The first decade of the 20th century saw impressive growth in travel to Estes Park. The splendid valley, previously accessible only by rugged dirt trails, was now a relatively smooth automobile drive away. By 1910, over 200,000 people lived in Denver, and Front Range towns like Boulder and Fort Collins were flourishing. Thousands of city dwellers, and quite a few out-of-state visitors, flocked to the beautiful peaks above Estes Park. Tourist lodges, private summer cabins, and new businesses spread throughout the region. "No matter which way you look," wrote a local paper, "you will see a new building going up."

Some locals, however, grew concerned with the pace of development. In September 1906, Freelan O. Stanley helped found the Estes Park Protective and Improvement Association. Among the organization's many goals was protecting the local environment. The group posted signs declaring, "You can keep Estes Park a beautiful wild garden. Spare the flowers! ... Those who pull flowers up by the roots will be condemned by all worthy people."

This dramatic shift in attitude encompassed far more than just wildflowers. After decades of unchecked resource extraction, the idea of protecting Colorado's natural resources had started to take root. On May 17, 1905, President Teddy Roosevelt created Medicine Bow Forest Reserve (later named Roosevelt National Forest), which encompassed 1.5 million acres of mountains, meadows, and lakes near Estes Park.

ENOS MILLS

Of all the early supporters of Rocky Mountain National Park, none is as famous as Enos Mills. His outdoor adventures and eloquent nature writing brought national attention to the Rocky Mountains, and his tireless efforts were vital to the creation of Colorado's most popular national park.

Born in Kansas in 1870, Enos Abijah Mills was a thin, sickly child. At age 14 he moved to Colorado and worked for his dad's cousin, the Rev. Elkanah Lamb, a fiery preacher who owned a lodge near Longs Peak and guided guests up the mountain. At 15, Mills climbed Longs Peak—an experience that left him with a passion for the region. He built a small cabin near the base of the mountain, then set off on an extended exploration of the Western United States.

In 1889, when he was 19 years old, Mills saw John Muir on a San Francisco beach. Mills introduced himself to the famous conservationist, who was then fighting for the creation of Yosemite National Park, and Muir invited him for a stroll through Golden Gate Park. Muir spoke passionately about the importance of wilderness conservation and implored Mills to visit America's great natural temples. The chance encounter left Mills transformed. He visited Yosemite and Yellowstone to see the new national parks first-hand—and dreamed of Colorado boasting its own national park. After brief stints working in Montana copper mines and attending business school, Mills returned to Colorado.

In 1902, Mills purchased Lamb's lodge and renamed it Longs Peak Inn. Just like Lamb, Mills guided guests to the top of Longs Peak, and he soon became one of the mountain's most prolific climbers. In August of 1906, Mills climbed Longs Peak 32 times, including six moonlight ascents. He also became the first person to climb Longs Peak in winter.

Mills worked as Colorado's first official "State Snow Observer," a job that required wandering Colorado's mountains during the winter to measure snowfall. During week-long snowshoe treks, Mills often subsisted off nothing but raisins. At one point he became snow-blind near the Continental Divide, then wandered so close to an avalanche that a blast of air knocked him over. Mills habitually put himself in dangerous situations, but he cherished the opportunity to explore the Rocky Mountains and observe their natural cycles.

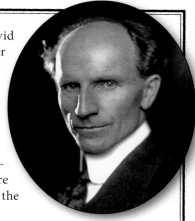

Despite limited schooling, Mills was an avid reader, and he began writing articles for Denver newspapers. Over time he developed into a gifted outdoor writer. As a naturalist, Mills' powers of observation were unmatched. He once counted 14,137 cones on a lodgepole pine. To learn more about beavers, he visited a beaver lodge daily for weeks, then wrote an entire book about it. Mills viewed nature as an interconnected whole. But he also believed it was more fun to know the biography of a single tree than the names of all the trees in the forest.

In 1906, Longs Peak Inn burned down. Mills rebuilt it as a grand, rustic lodge decorated with gnarled branches and fire-burnt logs. The new inn attracted a string of high-profile guests—Helen Keller, Frank Lloyd Wright, John D. Rockefeller, Jr.—but Mills was an unusually strict host. He expected visitors to study nature and get plenty of exercise, and he prohibited drinking, dancing, and card playing. While guiding, he always wore a suit. But Mills could also be playful and charming, and guests raved about their stay.

A trip to Switzerland showed Mills the vast economic potential of mountain tourism, and he felt Colorado could become the Switzerland of America—but only if citizens fought against the careless treatment of forests that plagued the Rockies for decades. Inspired by his hero, John Muir, Mills crisscrossed America giving public talks about the Rocky Mountains. He called Colorado's forests a "picturesque remnant and melancholy ruin of its former grandeur" and called for "an end to anarchy in the forests."

Mills caught the attention of President Teddy Roosevelt, who appointed him Government Lecturer on Forestry in 1907. By 1910, Mills had given over 2,000 lectures to schools, churches, and civic groups. Mills used his growing fame to push for permanent protection of Longs Peak and the mountains above Estes Park. He enlisted powerful allies, clashed with bureaucrats, antagonized neighbors, and rallied public support. But the hard work paid off. On January 26, 1915, Rocky Mountain became America's 13th national park.

Enos Mills died in 1922 at age 52 of blood poisoning from an infected tooth. He had authored 14 books, helped found the Colorado Mountain Club, and climbed Longs Peak nearly 300 times. Mills Lake, Mills Glacier, and Mills Moraine were named in his honor. Although Longs Peak Inn burned down in 1949, his small cabin still operates as a museum today (enosmills.com).

Mills called the creation of Rocky Mountain National Park "the proudest moment of my life." Today he is affectionately known as both the "John Muir of the Rockies" and the "Father of Rocky Mountain National Park."

In 1907, Herbert N. Wheeler became head of the Colorado Forest Service, and he recommended the creation of a 1,000-square-mile game refuge near Estes Park. The Estes Park Protective and Improvement Association enthusiastically embraced the idea. But Enos Mills, who had become a prominent wilderness advocate, vigorously opposed it. Although Mills also wanted the region protected, he didn't trust the National Forest Service, which allows mining, logging, and cattle grazing on its land. Mills believed the Forest Service "deals almost entirely with the business world and is as plainly and severely a business proposition as is the growing of wheat and potatoes."

Instead of a game refuge, Mills called for the creation of a 1,000-square-mile national park. The proposed park—"a scenic resource of enormous and exhaustless richness"—would prohibit mining, logging, and grazing, and thus protect the region's natural beauty forever. Mills persuaded the Estes Park Protective and Improvement Association to embrace his plan, then rallied public support for the cause. He gave lectures, courted the media, cajoled politicians, and gained the support of powerful civic organizations. Speaking to the Denver Chamber of Commerce, Mills proclaimed the time of the gun had passed and the automobile and camera had taken its place—a declaration that met with hearty applause.

Wheeler was taken aback. Not only would a new national park fall under the jurisdiction of the Department of Interior—and thus out of Wheeler's control—but it would lock up valuable natural resources. A small but vocal group of locals agreed. A handful of Mills' neighbors bitterly opposed a national park, and they formed a resistance group called the Front Range Settlers' League.

Mills denounced the Front Range Settlers' League and railed against the "aggressive and conspiratorial" Forest Service, claiming it was trying to "suppress and blackmail into silence any opposition to its methods." At one point Mills physically assaulted a member of a local ranching family whom Mills suspected of conspiring with the Forest Service to harass him.

Undeterred, Mills continued to fight for a national park. In 1912, he helped start the Colorado Mountain Club, which was modeled after the Sierra Club, an environmental advocacy group founded by his hero John Muir. The new organization became a valuable ally of the proposed park. The club's president, James Grafton Rogers, was a prominent Denver attorney with powerful connections. The CMC rallied support for the park and helped create improved maps of the region, which aided in drafting formal legislation.

In 1912, the Interior Department sent chief U.S. Geographer Robert Marshall to Colorado to evaluate the proposed national park. His report was ecstatic: "There is spread before the eye a gorgeous assemblage of wonderful mountain sculpture, surrounded by fantastic and everchanging clouds ... the whole presenting an impressive picture, never to be forgotten."

With Marshall's blessing, CMC president James Rogers drafted a national park bill, and Colorado Congressman Edward Taylor submitted it to Congress in February 1913. Complex land and water rights issues killed the bill twice, and five revisions reduced the proposed park to 359 square miles—one-third the original vision. Nevertheless, Enos Mills testified on Capitol Hill, Colorado politicians guided the bill through Congress, and on January 26, 1915, President Woodrow Wilson signed the bill into law. After years of effort, Rocky Mountain National Park became America's 13th national park.

The *Denver Post* ran a cartoon showing Enos Mills congratulated by Lady Colorado and her mountains. The paper also dubbed Mills the "Father of Rocky Mountain National Park." Later that year, on September 4, roughly 3,000 people gathered in Horseshoe Park to celebrate the creation of Rocky Mountain National Park. Enos Mills presided as master of ceremonies, reading a telegram from President Wilson. At one point a rainstorm drenched the crowd, but spirits were not dampened. The park's remarkable scenery was protected forever.

COLORADO — "ENOS, I'M PROUD OF YOU!"

A CENTURY OF PRESERVATION

It didn't take long for Rocky Mountain National Park to become one of America's most popular national parks. Located just 40 miles northwest of fast-growing Denver, "Rocky" attracted 31,000 visitors when it opened in 1915. Three years later, 117,000 people entered the park—more than Yellowstone, Yosemite, Glacier, and Crater Lake combined.

Despite booming visitation, the park participated in an unusual publicity stunt. On August 6, 1917, a barefoot 20-year-old college girl dressed in leopard skins said goodbye to Enos Mills and ran into the forest near Longs Peak. "Naked, Unarmed and Alone, 'Eve' Goes Forth Into Forest," blared a local newspaper. Over the next week, journalists breathlessly reported on Eve sightings in Colorado's own "Garden of Eden." Officials in Washington, D.C., were furious when they learned of the stunt, and park superintendent L. Claude Way dutifully apologized—even though he claimed it would bring "valuable publicity."

The incident revealed the opposing forces all national parks would struggle with over the next century. The fledgling National Park Service, created just one year earlier in 1916, needed visitors to justify its existence. Park Service director Stephen Mather built motor roads and grand rustic lodges in national parks, and he urged Americans to skip war-torn Europe and "See America First."

By 1920, Fall River Road stretched across Rocky Mountain National Park, crossing the Continental Divide and revealing the park's high-altitude wonderland. But the dirt road was rugged and steep—up to a 16 percent grade in places—so a modern paved road was commissioned. When Trail Ridge Road opened in 1932, it boasted a maximum grade of seven percent and showcased 11 miles above treeline. Topping out at 12,183 feet, it was the highest highway in the world.

Grand lodges were not built in Rocky Mountain National Park because multiple private lodges already existed within park boundaries. Moraine Park alone contained over a dozen buildings and a nine-hole golf course. Over the coming decades, however, the park purchased as many private inholdings as possible. Every lodge in the park was acquired and removed (to the dismay of many visitors), and by mid-century Moraine Park had largely returned to its natural state.

When Enos Mills initially proposed Rocky Mountain National Park, he hoped it would include both Pikes Peak and the Indian Peaks Wilderness south of the present-day park. His wish went unfulfilled, but in 1930 Rocky acquired 14,000 acres of Arapaho National Forest to the west, adding the Never Summer Mountains and Colorado River headwaters to the park.

As the century progressed, visitation continued to grow, topping one million visitors in 1948, two million in 1968, and three million in 1998. In 2015, Rocky Mountain National Park celebrated its Centennial, and visitation topped four million people for the first time.

THE FIRES OF 2020

In 2019, Rocky Mountain National Park recorded its most visits ever: 4.7 million, making it the third most popular national park in America. Then, barely three months into 2020, the COVID-19 pandemic led to an extended park closure. On March 20, Rocky Mountain National Park closed its gates for over two months. When the park reopened on May 27, visitors were required to wear masks, shuttles ran at reduced capacity, and a new timed-entry permit system was implemented for the first time. It was an unusual summer, but the biggest surprise was yet to come.

On August 13, a fire ignited near Chambers Lake and Cameron Peak, eight miles northwest of Rocky Mountain National Park. A multi-year drought left Colorado forests unusually dry, and a multi-decade mountain pine beetle outbreak (p.77) littered those same forests with millions of dead trees. Conditions were ripe for large, destructive fires. By September 6, the Cameron Peak fire burned over 20,000 acres. Over the next several days, hot temperatures and strong winds whipped up extreme conditions. The Cameron Peak fire grew to over 100,000 acres, including 7,000 acres in the northern portion of Rocky Mountain National Park. In a remarkable stroke of luck, an early snowstorm dropped nearly a foot of snow in the mountains, significantly dampening the fire. Within a week, however, the Cameron Peak fire was growing again, and by mid-October it had burned over 135,000 acres.

On October 14, another fire broke out roughly 30 miles southwest of Rocky Mountain National Park. The fire, named after nearby East Troublesome Creek, grew to 18,550 acres by October 20. Temperatures were unusually warm, and on October 21 wind gusts hit 60 mph. Within 24 hours, the East Troublesome fire exploded into one of the largest fires in Colorado history. At its peak the fire devoured 80 football fields per minute, burning 170,000 acres over three days. (Prior to 2020, Colorado's largest fire was 2002's Hayman Fire, which burned 137,760 acres over 40 days.) The East Troublesome fire created a pyrocumulonimbus cloud, which NASA describes as "the fire-breathing dragon of clouds ... an explosive storm cloud actually created by the smoke and heat from the fire." The apocalyptic cloud, which towered 40,000 feet above the Front Range and reached the stratosphere, cast a terrifying pall over Boulder. Within a few days, satellites detected smoke from the East Troublesome fire over Italy.

By the evening of October 21, the East Troublesome fire threatened Grand Lake, where firefighters battled to keep the blaze from engulfing the town. Just north of Grand Lake, the fire entered Rocky Mountain National Park and raced up Kawuneeche Valley. The western flank of the Front Range ignited, sending the fire towards the Continental Divide. A lack of fuels above treeline halted the fire's progress, but hot embers blew 1.5 miles across the Continental Divide, igniting a fire along Spruce Creek near Bear Lake. The East Troublesome fire was now burning on both sides of the Front Range. Firefighters battling the Cameron Peak fire, which had grown to over 200,000 acres, were dispatched to confront the new blaze. On October 22, Rocky Mountain National Park closed to the public for the second time in 2020, and the citizens of Estes Park evacuated. Over the next two days, strong winds hammered the fire, which split into two fingers that reached Moraine Park and Hollowell Park.

Then, on October 24, a cold front moved in and dumped snow on the fires, finally giving firefighters the upper hand. Rocky Mountain National Park reopened on November 6, and by early December the fires were fully contained. The Cameron Peak fire burned 208,663 acres—the largest fire in Colorado history. The East Troublesome fire burned 193,812 acres—the second largest fire in Colorado history. A third 2020 fire, the Pine Gulch fire north of Grand Junction, burned 139,007 acres—the third largest fire in Colorado history. By the end of 2020, over 800,000 acres had burned in Colorado, and the cost of fighting those fires exceeded $260 million. The Cameron Peak and East Troublesome fires destroyed hundreds of structures and resulted in the death of an elderly couple that refused to leave their home near Grand Lake. As of this writing, the cause of both fires remains unknown.

Rocky Mountain National Park suffered roughly 30,000 acres of fire damage, impacting roughly nine percent of the park. Prior to 2020, the park's largest fire had been 2012's Fern Lake fire, which burned 3,500 acres. Moving forward, the National Park Service will continue its policy of periodic prescribed burns and reducing forest fuels to minimize the threat of future fires.

MORAINE PARK

THIS GLACIALLY SCULPTED meadow is one of the highlights of Rocky Mountain National Park. Few places in America showcase such compelling Ice Age geology—and few are quite so lovely. Surrounded by snow-capped peaks in spring, filled with wildflowers in summer, echoing with elk in autumn, and hinting at its frozen glacial past in winter, there's never a bad time to visit.

Yet many visitors drive past Moraine Park on a mad dash to find parking at Bear Lake. Others become "trapped" here during peak-season when the park closes the road to Bear Lake due to traffic jams. Were it not for the elusive lure of limited parking, however, many people might be perfectly content to spend time in Moraine Park. There are great hiking trails, terrific horseback tours (p.25), and excellent wildlife watching. Best of all, this enormous meadow—the size of 360 football fields—has lots of space to spread outs.

Moraine Park is also a great place to witness one of the wildlife highlights of Rocky Mountain National Park. During the annual elk rut in autumn, dominant bulls assemble large harems of females. The sight of these powerful animals—and the sound of their haunting bugle—is all the more remarkable in a setting as majestic as Moraine Park.

A short distance north of Moraine Park lies Beaver Meadows (p.137). Though not as physically dramatic as Moraine Park, Beaver Meadows is also a good place to look for birds and other wildlife. Leisurely hiking trails twist through Upper and Lower Beaver Meadows, where abundant aspen radiate autumn gold.

From late May to mid-October, a free shuttle loops around popular stops in Moraine Park, traveling as far south as Sprague Lake (p.155). The shuttle also stops at Park & Ride, where you can catch another shuttle to Bear Lake's most popular trailheads. So slow down and relax. Even if you move at a glacial pace in the morning, there's no reason not to enjoy Moraine Park.

BEST HIKES

DEER MOUNTAIN 142   **CUB LAKE 144**

FERN LAKE 146

Beaver Meadows Visitor Center

Located one mile east of Rocky Mountain National Park's most popular entrance, this is one of the park's most popular visitor centers. Inside you'll find a ranger-staffed help desk, a store run by the Rocky Mountain Conservancy, and a theater that plays a short film about the park. Adjacent to the main building is the best bathroom for miles. (If you don't enjoy stinky pit toilets, you should seriously consider taking advantage of Estes Park's municipal water supply before entering the park.) Behind the visitor center is a Wilderness Office where you can pick up reserved backpacking permits. There are also a handful of picnic tables around the visitor center, but there are much prettier picnic areas in the park.

Beaver Meadows Visitor Center was designed by Taliesin West Architects, which was founded by Frank Lloyd Wright. Although Wright died before the building was commissioned, his apprentice, Thomas Casey, was its lead architect. The visitor center is angular and geometric—hallmarks of Wright's iconic style—and sandstone helps it blend in with the natural surroundings. The building's most intricate designs, inspired by Native American artwork, are made of Corten steel that rusts to a beautiful reddish-brown, forming a protective coating that requires no paint. The visitor center was part of the National Park Service's Mission 66 initiative, which aimed to modernize national parks for the agency's 50th birthday in 1966. Beaver Meadows Visitor Center opened in 1967, and it was declared a National Historic Landmark in 2001.

The Beaver

Longs Peak

Beaver Meadows

These peaceful meadows aren't nearly as dramatic as Moraine Park, but they are a great place to escape the crowds. A network of easy trails passes through Upper and Lower Beaver Meadows, which were named after Beaver Brook, which flows down from Beaver Mountain. You'd be forgiven for thinking this is a good place to spot beavers (p.102), but those fascinating creatures generally prefer other parts of the park. The most reliable beaver sighting is eight miles south and 6,000 feet up. There, near the summit of Longs Peak, you can see (with a little imagination) a stone beaver climbing the left side of the mountain. This anthropomorphic ascent was noted by James Michener in his novel *Centennial*, which celebrated Colorado's 100th anniversary. As you drive through Rocky Mountain National Park, always keep an eye out for the stone beaver climbing Longs Peak.

Moraine Park

This enormous meadow, 1.5 miles long by half-a-mile wide, is a glorious example of the park's glacial past. During the Ice Age, when dozens of glaciers descended from the Front Range, multiple glaciers converged to form the Thompson Glacier, which flowed into Moraine Park. As the 1,500-foot-thick glacier flowed east, it acted like an enormous conveyor belt, depositing debris to each side to form what geologist call lateral moraines. At the glacier's furthest extent, roughly 18,000 years ago, a terminal moraine formed at the front of the glacier near the east end of Moraine Park. When the ice melted, a large lake formed between the moraines, and over time sediment and organic debris settled to form a flat lake bottom. Water erosion eventually cut through the terminal moraine, draining the lake and leaving this beautiful, flat meadow behind.

South Lateral Moraine

Today the sunny south slope of North Lateral Moraine is home to ponderosa pines, which prefer drier soils, while the shadier north slope of South Lateral Moraine has a mix of lodgepole pines and Douglas-fir, which prefer moister soils. The Big Thompson River flows through the center of Moraine Park, nourishing a lush riparian habitat. Fences protect riverside vegetation from overgrazing by elk and deer. Visitors can enter these fenced-in areas through metal gates to hike or fish along the riverbank. Easy hiking trails also skirt the southern and western edges of Moraine Park.

When elk (p.94) descend from the park's higher elevations in autumn, Moraine Park is one of their favorite gathering places. Multiple pullouts along Moraine Park Road and Fern Lake Road are good places to safely view them from a distance. During the elk rut in September and October, foot traffic is not allowed in Moraine Park from 5pm to 10am.

Moraine Park Discovery Center

Perched 100 feet above Moraine Park between North Lateral Moraine and Terminal Moraine, Moraine Park Discovery Center offers a terrific perspective on the dramatic surroundings. The historic building, constructed in 1923 out of ponderosa logs and local rocks, is open late spring through mid-fall. Downstairs there's a small store run by Rocky Mountain Conservancy. Upstairs you'll find exhibits exploring the region's natural and human history, plus great views from large picture windows. Outside an easy 0.6-mile interpretive trail loops around the building, passing five stops with benches, interpretive signs, and scenic views. Steps at the north end of the parking area lead to an outdoor amphitheater that sometimes hosts ranger programs.

Today Moraine Park is wild and natural. In the 1900s, however, there were dozens of buildings in the meadow, including lodges, private cabins, a post office, and a nine-hole golf course. Other than bustling Estes Park, Moraine Park was the largest town for miles. After the creation of Rocky Mountain National Park, most buildings were purchased and removed. Today only a few historic buildings remain, including Moraine Park Discovery Center, which once served as a tearoom and dancehall for the Moraine Lodge. A nearby cabin was the summer home of Pulitzer Prize-winning journalist William Allen White—best known for his 1896 editorial "What's The Matter With Kansas"—and today it houses the park's visiting artist-in-residence. A handful of private cabins remain scattered around the edges of Moraine Park.

⤳ DEER MOUNTAIN ↝

SUMMARY Rising 1,500 feet above the north end of Beaver Meadows, Deer Mountain is my favorite moderate hike in the Moraine Park region. From the summit you'll enjoy fabulous views extending from Estes Park to the Front Range peaks along the Continental Divide. From Deer Mountain Trailhead you'll rise through classic ponderosa forest, enjoying striking views of Longs Peak along the way. After a steep climb through aspen and lodgepole pine—with occasional views of the Mummy Range to the northwest—the trail flattens out and descends roughly half-a-mile before embarking on its final ascent. A quarter-mile spur trail branches off to the summit, where rocky outcrops make great natural viewpoints. If you bring food to the summit, you might wonder why this mountain isn't named Aggressive Hungry Chipmunk Mountain. (Please don't feed the chipmunks!) The name Deer Mountain first appeared in Frederick Chapin's 1889 book *Mountaineering in Colorado.*

TRAILHEAD (Elevation: 8,930') Deer Mountain Trailhead is located at the junction of U.S. 36 and U.S. 34, near the start of Trail Ridge Road.

TRAIL INFO

RATING Moderate	**DISTANCE** 6.2 miles, round-trip
HIKING TIME 4 hours	**ELEVATION CHANGE** 1,007 feet

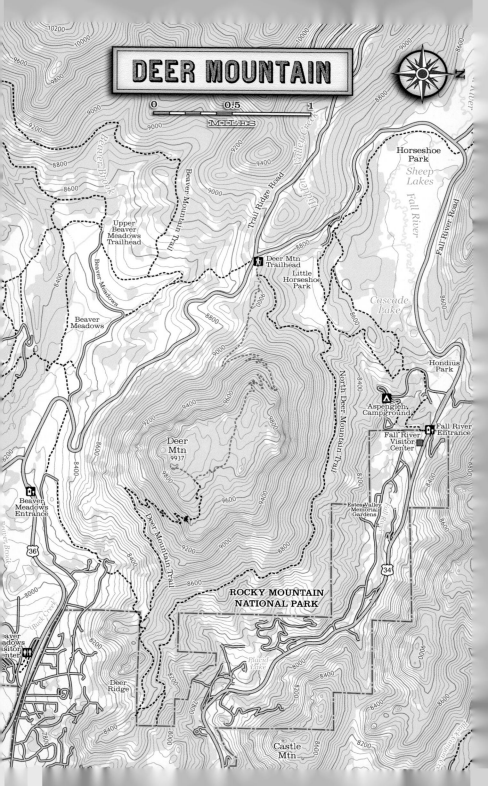

◅ CUB LAKE ⤚

SUMMARY This small, lovely lake isn't the most dramatic destination in Rocky Mountain National Park. But the moderate hike to Cub Lake is a nice, family-friendly option with opportunities to view wildlife. Much of this area burned during the 2012 Fern Lake Fire, and today the vegetation continues to recover. From Cub Lake Trailhead you'll skirt the northwest edge of Moraine Park (where elk sometimes browse), pass a series of beaver ponds (where moose sometimes graze), and rise through a lush aspen grove (where deer sometimes browse). After a short climb you'll reach Cub Lake, where yellow pond-lilies bloom in July and August. The northern shore has several nice viewpoints where you can admire Stones Peak in the distance. After enjoying the scenery, return the way you came. Or, if you'd like a longer hike, continue 0.9 miles to The Pool (a deep section of the Big Thompson River), bear right, and follow Fern Lake Trail 1.7 miles to Fern Lake Trailhead, which lies one mile west of Cub Lake Trailhead.

TRAILHEAD (Elevation: 8,080') Cub Lake Trailhead is located 1.2 miles down Fern Lake Road, which starts just before Moraine Park Campground.

◆ TRAIL INFO ◆

RATING Moderate	**DISTANCE** 4.6 miles, round-trip
HIKING TIME 3–4 hours	**ELEVATION GAIN** 540 feet

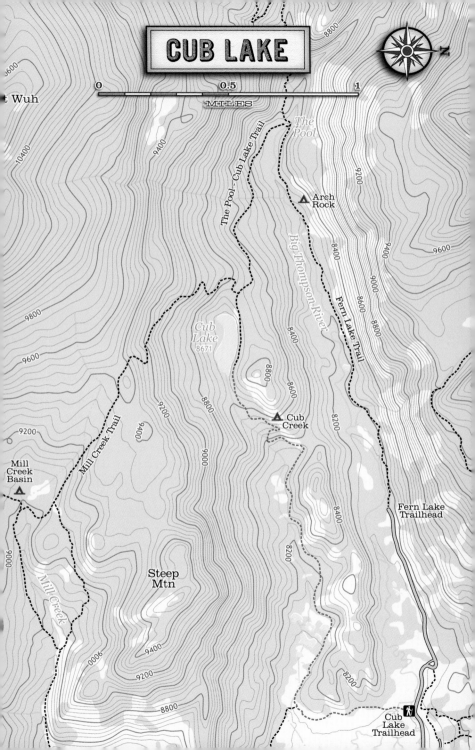

~⊲ FERN LAKE ⊳~

SUMMARY This is one of the top hikes in the Moraine Park region, passing beautiful sights along Big Thompson River en route to gorgeous Fern Lake. Sadly, parts of the route burned during the 2020 East Troublesome Fire, and it will be years before the trail regains its full glory. If you don't mind hiking through charred forest, start your adventure at Fern Lake Trailhead and follow Fern Lake Trail as it parallels Big Thompson River. Beyond The Pool—a swirling, deep water section near the confluence of Big Thompson River, Fern Creek, and Spruce Creek—the trail rises above Fern Creek, passes Fern Fall, and continues to Fern Lake. A footbridge on the lake's northern shore offers striking views of the surrounding peaks, including Notchtop Mountain and Little Matterhorn (named for its resemblance to the Swiss mountain). Strong hikers can hike one additional mile to gorgeous Odessa Lake. From Odessa Lake it's 4.1 miles to Bear Lake, where seasonal shuttles can bring you back to Fern Lake Trailhead.

TRAILHEAD (Elevation: 8,155') Fern Lake Trailhead is located at the end of Fern Lake Road, which starts just before Moraine Park Campground.

TRAIL INFO

RATING Strenuous	**DISTANCE** 7.6 miles, round-trip
HIKING TIME 5 hours	**ELEVATION GAIN** 1,373 feet

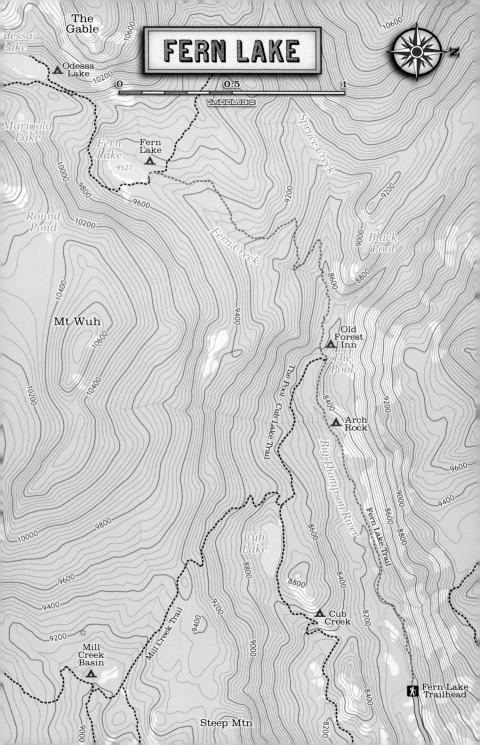

BEAR LAKE

THE BEAR LAKE region is one of the most popular destinations in Rocky Mountain National Park—and for good reason. Nestled directly below rugged Front Range peaks, this alpine wonderland provides easy access to pristine lakes, beautiful waterfalls, and miles of fabulous hiking trails. From casual shoreline strolls to strenuous all-day treks to the Continental Divide, there's a hike for everyone here.

The only downside: congestion. Bear Lake is located at the end of a nine-mile road that climbs 1,400 feet above Moraine Park. There's only one way in, and one way out, and that can be problematic when things get crowded. During peak season the road's most popular parking areas—Bear Lake, Glacier Gorge, Bierstadt Lake—often fill to capacity before 6am. On most summer days, and most weekends in autumn, winter and spring, *all* of the region's parking areas fill to capacity, at which point the park temporarily closes Bear Lake Road past Moraine Park until congestion diminishes.

But relax. You don't need to wake up at the crack of dawn to enjoy Bear Lake. If you can suppress your *must-find-a-great-parking-spot* instincts, there are several easy ways to visit Bear Lake stress-free—even during peak season. One option is driving to Park & Ride, a large parking area along Bear Lake Road where free shuttles to Bear Lake depart. Another is catching the free seasonal shuttle that loops between Estes Park and Park & Ride. A third option is camping at Glacier Basin Campground or Moraine Park Campground, which are both serviced by park shuttles. (All of these options are detailed on page 151.)

Bear Lake is also terrific off-season. Autumn brings stunning foliage to the mountains around Glacier Gorge, and the landscape is magical after a fresh dusting of snow. Bear Lake Road is open in winter, making it a favorite destination for winter hikers, snowshoers, and cross-country skiers.

BEST HIKES

EMERALD LAKE 158

LAKE HAIYAHA 162

ALBERTA FALLS 164

SKY POND 168

BIERSTADT LAKE 170

FLATTOP MTN. 172

Glacier Basin Campground

Getting Around Bear Lake

Due to Bear Lake's popularity, the region's limited trailside parking areas often fill by 6 am. Fortunately, there are several alternate ways to access this area, even when Bear Lake Road is closed to private vehicles.

PARK & RIDE

Three miles northeast of Bear Lake is a large "Park & Ride" that serves as the hub for the park's three shuttle routes. An adjacent parking area offers over 300 parking spaces. Free shuttles to Bierstadt Lake, Glacier Gorge Trailhead, and Bear Lake depart Park & Ride every 10–15 minutes from late May to mid-October. During peak season, Park & Ride's parking area often fills to capacity, at which point the park closes private vehicle access to Bear Lake Road beyond Moraine Park. Bear Lake Road closures often occur in late morning and early afternoon.

ESTES PARK SHUTTLE

When Bear Lake Road is closed to private vehicles, you can still catch a free seasonal shuttle to Park & Ride from Estes Park (p.47). The shuttle normally runs from late May to mid-October.

GLACIER BASIN CAMPGROUND

One of the best ways to experience the Bear Lake region is camping at Glacier Basin Campground (p.38), located across the road from Park & Ride. Glacier Basin Campground is on the Moraine Park Shuttle route.

Former
Skid Trail

Holowell Park

Tuxedo Park

Tuxedo Park

Most visitors drive past this creekside picnic area, located 1.5 miles beyond Moraine Park, but it's my favorite picnic area along Bear Lake Road. From the small parking area, stone steps descend to a flat area with half a dozen picnic tables under tall, shady pines. Glacier Creek flows alongside the picnic area, adding a relaxing natural soundtrack. The name Tuxedo Park comes from the 1920s and 1930s, when visitors from the nearby YMCA of the Rockies donned tuxedos and elegant dresses for elaborate picnics here. Today's attire is considerably more relaxed.

Hollowell Park

Nestled in a small grove of ponderosa pines, Hollowell Park is another great picnic area en route to Bear Lake. In autumn, golden aspen reveal a former logging skid trail on the north side of Bierstadt Moraine. In 1907, a sawmill on top of Bierstadt Moraine cut logs into lumber, which was hauled down the skid trail to build The Stanley Hotel in Estes Park. Over the past century, sun-loving aspen slowly reclaimed the once barren trail.

During the Great Depression, Hollowell Park hosted a Civilian Conservation Corps (CCC) tent camp. The CCC was a New Deal program that provided government jobs to young, unemployed men. Workers in Rocky Mountain National Park earned $1 a day building trails, roads, bridges, and other infrastructure.

Thatchtop
12,668'

Taylor
Peak
13,153'

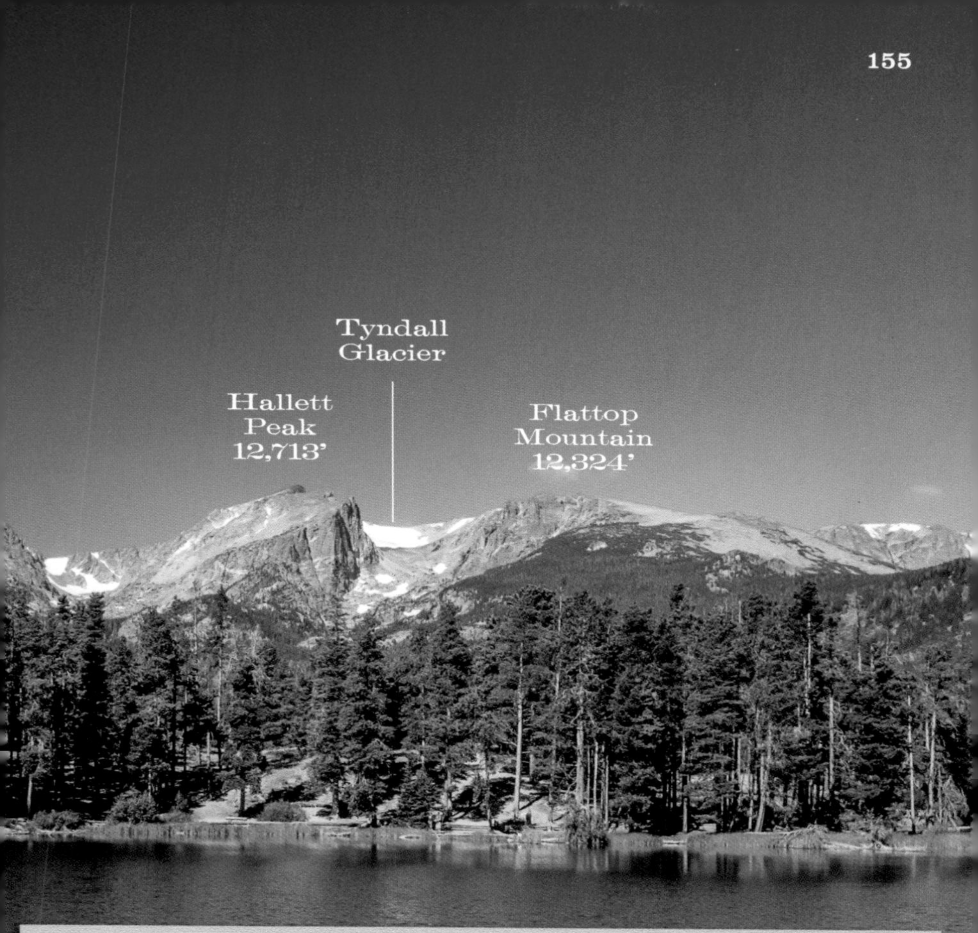

Tyndall
Glacier

Hallett
Peak
12,713'

Flattop
Mountain
12,324'

Sprague Lake

Although less famous than Bear Lake, many visitors find Sprague Lake equally beautiful. An easy 0.5-mile accessible path loops around the lovely shore, located 8,710 feet above sea level. There are plenty of great views, but my favorite is from a sturdy wooden viewing platform on the northeast shore. From there you can see half a dozen Front Range peaks piercing the western horizon. The Arapaho call Hallett Peak "Thunder Peak" for the thunderclouds that often hang over its summit. In 1887, mountaineer Frederick Chapin named the peak after his guide, William Hallett. Strong hikers can summit Hallett Peak after climbing Flattop Mountain (p.172). Between Hallett and Flattop lies Tyndall Glacier (p.175), one of several small glaciers that remain in Rocky Mountain National Park.

Unlike Bear Lake, which was sculpted by glaciers, Sprague Lake is manmade. In the early 1900s, local innkeeper Abner Sprague dammed Boulder Brook to create a trout fishing lake for his guests. Today a spur trail leads from Sprague Lake to the park's only wheelchair-accessible wilderness campsite, reservable through the park's Wilderness Office.

Half
Mountain

Longs
Peak

Glacier
Gorge

Flattop
Mountain

Bear Lake

This pristine lake, located 9,475 feet above sea level, is one of the most popular destinations in the park. An easy 0.6-mile accessible trail loops around the shore, where wooden benches offer great viewpoints. From the lake's northern shore you'll enjoy bold views of Longs Peak (p.196) towering above Glacier Gorge—a scene memorialized on Colorado's state quarter. The jagged peaks to the right of Longs Peak are the Keyboard of the Winds. When strong winds blow, these peaks are said to emit an eerie sound. Flattop Mountain (p.172), covered in tawny alpine tundra, rises above the lake's western shore to the Continental Divide. Numbered signs along Bear Lake Nature Trail correspond to a self-guided nature booklet sold near the trailhead. The name Bear Lake comes from a bear sighting here in the late 1800s, but today bear sightings are extremely rare. From 1921 to 1959, the rustic Bear Lake Lodge hosted guests on the lake's southern shore. Guests often stayed for weeks or months, but the park removed the lodge in favor of a more natural landscape.

COLORADO
1876

COLORFUL COLORADO
2006
E PLURIBUS UNUM

⊰ EMERALD LAKE ⊱

SUMMARY This gorgeous alpine lake, situated over 10,000 feet above sea level and surrounded by dramatic peaks, is one of the park's most popular hikes. The trail to Emerald Lake passes through classic Rocky Mountain scenery, visiting Nymph Lake and Dream Lake along the way. If you don't mind the steady stream of hikers, it might be the best moderate hike in the park. From the trailhead, hike 0.5 miles to Nymph Lake, which is named after the yellow pond lilies (original scientific name *Nymphaea polysepala*) that dot its surface. Continue 0.6 miles to Dream Lake, where the sharp profile of Hallett Peak towers to the west. The trail continues along Dream Lake's northern shore—look for greenback cutthroat trout (p.103) in the water—then rises alongside wildflower-strewn Tyndall Creek en route to Emerald Lake. Nestled in Tyndall Gorge, Emerald Lake's pristine waters are fed by Tyndall Glacier (p.175), which lies between Hallett Peak and Flattop Mountain (p.172).

TRAILHEAD (Elevation: 9,475') Bear Lake Trailhead is located at Bear Lake Parking Area, next to the shuttle stop.

TRAIL INFO

RATING Moderate	**DISTANCE** 3.6 miles, round-trip
HIKING TIME 2 hours	**ELEVATION GAIN** 657 feet

Both Nymph Lake (left) and Dream Lake (above) formed due to a retreating Ice Age glacier. As temperatures warmed, the glacier retreated in fits and starts, occasionally pausing in places. When the glacier paused, ice continued to flow like a conveyor belt, depositing rocks and debris at the front to form a terminal moraine. After the glacier melted, two terminal moraines dammed Tyndall Creek to create Nymph Lake and Dream Lake.

⊰ LAKE HAIYAHA ⊱

SUMMARY This beautiful lake (pronounced hi-YA-ha, Arapaho for "big rocks") is a terrific alternative to Emerald Lake that attracts far fewer crowds. From Bear Lake Trailhead, follow the same route toward Emerald Lake, passing Nymph Lake en route to Dream Lake. Just before Dream Lake, you'll zig where others zag, heading south to Chaos Canyon. Don't let the name deter you. The hike to Chaos Canyon passes through beautiful forest with great views of Bear Lake and Nymph Lake to the northeast. Longs Peak towers above Glacier Gorge to the southeast. The most chaotic part is at the very end, when you'll scramble over a jumble of *haiyahas* to reach the shore. Find a flat rock to sit down and relax, then enjoy the epic Rocky Mountain scenery reflected in the lake's deep green water. If you don't mind hiking one extra mile on your return, you can make a loop by heading east at Lake Haiyaha junction, hiking past Alberta Falls (p.164), then bearing left to return to Bear Lake.

TRAILHEAD (Elevation: 9,475') Bear Lake Trailhead is located at Bear Lake Parking Area, next to the shuttle stop.

TRAIL INFO

RATING Moderate   **DISTANCE** 4.2 miles, round-trip

HIKING TIME 3 hours   **ELEVATION CHANGE** 745 feet

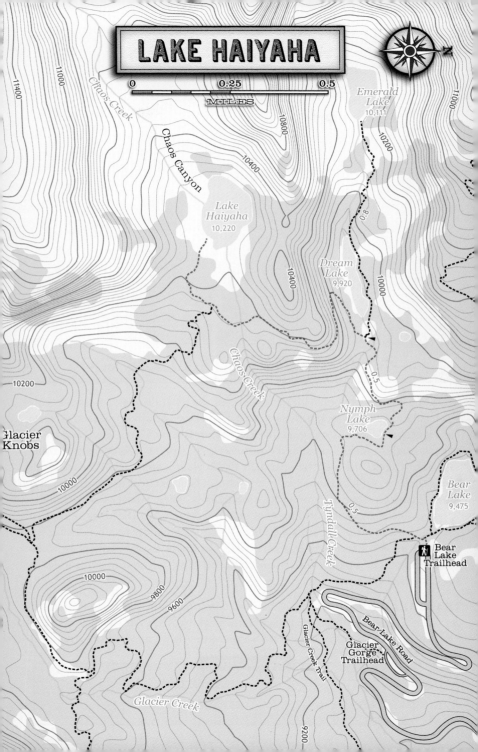

⇜ ALBERTA FALLS ⇝

SUMMARY This popular hike visits one of the most dramatic and accessible waterfalls in Rocky Mountain National Park. The most direct route to Alberta Falls starts at Glacier Gorge Parking Area. From Glacier Gorge Trailhead you'll pass through beautiful forest and cross a series of wooden footbridges en route to Glacier Creek. The trail then parallels the creek as it approaches the waterfall. Along the way you'll be treated to lovely views of Glacier Creek as it cascades past aspen groves. A wooden sign marks Alberta Falls, where Glacier Creek tumbles 25 feet over the rocks, generating cool mist in spring when the creek is swollen with snowmelt. Early homesteader Abner Sprague named this waterfall after his wife. The hike to Alberta Falls is particularly dramatic in late September, when golden aspen light up the trail. Past Alberta Falls, the trail continues 2.2 miles to The Loch (see following page).

TRAILHEAD (Elevation: 9,175') The most common route to Alberta Falls starts at Glacier Gorge Trailhead at Glacier Gorge Parking Area. An alternate route to Alberta Falls, just 0.1 mile longer one-way, starts at Bear Lake Parking Area.

TRAIL INFO

RATING Easy	**DISTANCE** 1.6 miles, round-trip
HIKING TIME 1 hour	**ELEVATION GAIN** 219 feet

Taylor Glacier

The Loch

This large alpine lake, located 2.2 miles past Alberta Falls, makes a great destination for strong hikers. From the eastern shore you'll enjoy stunning views of the Cathedral Wall, which stands guard before two glaciers: Andrews Glacier (to the right) and Taylor Glacier (to the left). During the Ice Age, these glaciers converged to form Loch Vale Glacier, which carved this dramatic U-shaped valley. When the glaciers melted the valley flooded, creating The Loch. The lake was originally named after a Kansas banker named Locke, but Abner Sprauge changed the spelling to the Scottish word Loch, which means "Lake Valley."

Cathedral Wall

Andrews Glacier

❧ SKY POND ❧

SUMMARY Rising over 1,600 feet to one of the park's most dramatic bodies of water, Sky Pond is my favorite strenuous hike in the Bear Lake region. It offers similar scenery to Emerald Lake—wildflower-strewn rivers, waterfalls, alpine lakes—but on an even grander scale. From Glacier Gorge Trailhead you'll hike 0.8 miles to Alberta Falls (p.164), then continue 2.2 miles to The Loch (p.166). This route is particularly beautiful in late September, when the aspen are golden. After passing the northern shore of The Loch, you'll follow Icy Brook and climb dramatic stone steps above treeline. The trail's most formidable obstacle is a steep scramble up wet rocks next to Timberline Falls. From there you'll hike past the beautiful Lake of Glass, passing through a thicket of vegetation to Sky Pond. The Sharkstooth pinnacles pierce the northwest horizon, while the rugged spine of the Continental Divide rises above Taylor Glacier to the southwest.

TRAILHEAD (Elevation: 9,240') The most popular route to Sky Pond starts at Glacier Gorge Trailhead at Glacier Gorge Parking Area. An alternate route, just 0.1 mile longer one-way, starts at Bear Lake Parking Area.

TRAIL INFO

RATING Strenuous	**DISTANCE** 9.8 miles, round-trip
HIKING TIME 6 hours	**ELEVATION GAIN** 1,660 feet

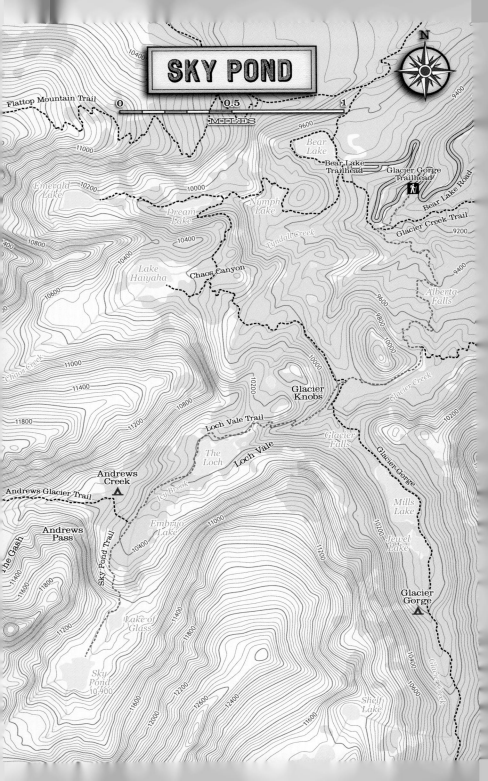

⊰ BIERSTADT LAKE ⊱

SUMMARY Bierstadt Lake was named after one of America's most famous landscape painters (p.120), and it's easy to see why. Nestled on top of Bierstadt Moraine—an enormous ridge deposited by glaciers 20,000 years ago—the lake's western shore frames a stunning view of Front Range peaks. Reflected in the water, the parade of mountains forms one of the most impressive views in the park. From Bierstadt Lake Trailhead you'll switchback nearly 600 feet up Bierstadt Moraine, enjoying panoramic views of the Bear Lake region below. In early October, when the aspen peak, this is one of the best foliage hikes in the park. On top of Bierstadt Moraine you'll reach a junction. Bear right to visit Bierstadt Lake's eastern shore, where you can enjoy the famous view from a lovely sand beach. The trail loops around the lake and returns to the junction, from which you'll hike back to the trailhead, enjoying glorious views along the way.

TRAILHEAD (Elevation: 8,850') The trail starts from tiny Bierstadt Lake Parking Area, which is nearly always full. Better to park at Park and Ride and catch the free shuttle to the trailhead.

◣ TRAIL INFO ▶

RATING Moderate	**DISTANCE** 3.1 miles, round-trip
HIKING TIME 2 hours	**ELEVATION GAIN** 604 feet

⊸ FLATTOP MOUNTAIN ᠎

SUMMARY Flattop Mountain is one of the most challenging hikes in the Bear Lake region—but with great effort comes great reward. Topping out at 12,324 feet (nearly 3,000 feet above Bear Lake), Flattop Mountain straddles the Continental Divide and offers panoramic views from the heart of the park. The trail to the summit was originally used by native tribes, who hunted elk on Flattop Mountain (p.106). From Bear Lake the Flattop Mountain Trail rises above Tyndall Gorge, passing dramatic overlooks high above Dream Lake and Emerald Lake. The views become even more expansive as you rise above treeline into sparse alpine tundra. On the summit you'll enjoy epic views over the Continental Divide into the heart of the Rockies. Tyndall Glacier lies just south of Flattop Mountain near the top of Tyndall Gorge. If skies are clear, consider hiking 0.75 miles to Hallett Peak, whose 12,713-foot summit offers even better views.

TRAILHEAD (Elevation: 9,475') The hike starts at the Bear Lake Parking area, next to the shuttle stop. The trail to Flattop Mountain veers off the Bear Lake Trail on the northeastern shore of Bear Lake.

TRAIL INFO

RATING Strenuous	**DISTANCE** 8.5 miles, round-trip
HIKING TIME 6 hours	**ELEVATION GAIN** 2,850 feet

Longs
Peak

Emerald Lake

Tyndall Glacier

Lying between Hallett Peak and Flattop Mountain, Tyndall Glacier is one of eight named glaciers that remain in Rocky Mountain National Park. During the Ice Age, around 18,000 years ago, a far larger glacier flowed down from this spot, but it melted several thousand years later. Tyndall Glacier is the remnant of a relatively recent glacial advance that started around 4,000 years ago. The glacier reached its peak roughly 150 years ago, then receded until the 1940s. Although it grew from the 1940s through the 1990s, it receded over the past two decades. Tyndall Glacier is named after John Tyndall, a 19th-century scientist and alpinist who studied glaciers and discovered the greenhouse effect. Today his namesake glacier moves so slowly that it barely qualifies as a glacier.

Hallett
Peak

Mount Meeker & Long's Peak

LONGS PEAK & WILD BASIN

THERE ARE MANY prominent peaks in Rocky Mountain National Park, but one towers above all others: 14,259-foot Longs Peak. The highest peak in the park beckons mountain climbers from around the world. A rugged seven-mile trail rises to The Keyhole, and from there it's a challenging 1.5-mile climb to the summit. Those who make it to the top enjoy panoramic views across northern Colorado. Far more than a hike, Longs Peak is Rocky Mountain National Park's most famous adventure.

Longs Peak dominates the southeast corner of the park, but it's hardly the only attraction here. Two entrances, Longs Peak and Wild Basin, offer access to some of the best hiking trails in the park. Trails range from easy strolls to moderate hikes to rugged overnight backpacks. The dramatic landscape, which includes pristine lakes and beautiful waterfalls, shelters some of the most impressive scenery in the park. Visitors come here to bask in the rugged drama of the park's tallest peaks, enjoying maximum natural beauty even if it means a minimum of creature comforts. This was true when Enos Mills, the father of Rocky Mountain National Park (p.124), built a cabin near the base of Longs Peak, and it remains true today.

Both Longs Peak Ranger Station and Wild Basin are located off Highway 7, which stretches 34 miles from Estes Park to the small town of Lyons. The drive features gorgeous views of Longs Peak, Twin Sisters, and Mount Meeker. You'll also pass a handful of shops, galleries, and historic cabins along the way. The most famous roadside attraction is the fairytale Chapel on the Rock (p.182), one of Colorado's most beautiful churches.

BEST HIKES

The Old Gallery

Highway 7

This two-lane highway heads south from Estes Park, parallels the eastern boundary of Rocky Mountain National Park, and drops into South Saint Vrain Canyon en route to the small town of Lyons. Although sparsely populated, the 16-mile stretch between Estes Park and Allenspark, a tiny town near the southern tip of the park, has several interesting sights along the way.

Seven Keys Lodge (formerly Baldpate Inn) is a century-old lodge located near Lily Lake (p.180). It boasts the world's largest public key collection—roughly 30,000 keys dangle from the ceiling and walls—and a cozy dining room that serves lunch and dinner (4900 Hwy. 7, 970-586-6151).

The **Enos Mills Cabin** is the former home of Enos Mills, the father of Rocky Mountain National Park. Built by Enos in 1885, the rustic cabin is owned by his descendants, who maintain it as a museum. Private tours are available by appointment. Located eight miles south of Estes Park (enosmills.com).

Eagle Plume's Gallery has an extensive collection of exquisite Native American art, crafts, and jewelry from across North America. Live artist events are held in summer (9853 Hwy. 7, eagle-plumes.com).

The Old Gallery is an Allenspark non-profit community center that hosts art exhibitions, concerts, classes, lectures, and special events throughout the year (14863 Hwy. 7, theoldgallery.org).

Mountain Meadow Cafe serves hearty breakfasts, baked goods, sandwiches, burgers, and weekend BBQs (441 Business Hwy. 7, 303-747-2541).

Lily Lake

Perched exactly 9,000 feet above sea level, this roadside lake is one of the most beautiful and accessible sights along Highway 7. It's located seven miles south of Estes Park and 2.5 miles north of the turnoff to Longs Peak Ranger Station. From the parking area, an easy, 0.8-mile wheelchair-accessible trail wraps around Lily Lake. The slightly more challenging Lily Ridge Trail is a 0.4-mile spur trail that offers elevated views above the northern shore. Lily Ridge Trail branches off the main trail near the eastern shore and reconnects at the western shore. No matter which route you choose, you'll enjoy captivating views of Longs Peak looming above the southern horizon.

The Arapaho call this lake *habas (sh)-hokgóy(sh)*, "Beaver Lodge." White settlers dubbed it Lake of the Lilies because water lilies once grew here. It was a favorite destination of Enos Mills, who loved observing the many animals that frequented the lake. In 1915, engineers dammed the lake to create a reservoir, and the new lake became too deep for water lilies.

Chapel on the Rock

There are lots of gorgeous views along Highway 7, but this fairy-tale church offers one of the best. Perched on a natural rock outcrop in front of massive Mount Meeker, Chapel on the Rock (officially St. Catherine of Siena Chapel) is one of the most beautiful churches in Colorado. Its story began in 1917, when Monsignor Joseph Bosetti, Archdiocese of Denver, searched for a meteor he saw while camping. Bosetti never found the meteor, but he did discover this beautiful rock outcrop. Inspired by the Bible passage "Upon this rock I will build my church," (Matthew 16:18) Bosetti devoted himself to construction of the chapel,

which opened in 1936. When Pope John Paul II visited Colorado in 1993, he came to Chapel on the Rock to pray, hike, and bask in the dramatic mountain scenery. In 2013, a landslide triggered by floods destroyed many of the surrounding buildings, but the chapel survived. Renovations, including a new Pope John Paul II Memorial Trail, are still underway. Catholic Mass is hosted every Friday at 8:30am. Visitors are welcome to visit the chapel's beautiful interior and browse the gift shop. The adjacent Heritage Center explores the history of the chapel. Chapel on the Rock is extremely popular for Catholic weddings, with reservations often booked up to a year in advance. Open 10am to 4pm, Tuesday through Sunday (campstmalo.org).

⌁ TWIN SISTERS ⌁

SUMMARY These craggy twin peaks, which lie directly across Tahosa Valley from Longs Peak, offer spectacular views of the Front Range as it marches across the western horizon. Although classified as a moderate hike, Twin Sisters has over 2,000 feet of vertical elevation change, so be prepared for a workout. From the trailhead you'll rise through a majestic lodgepole pine forest as you ascend the western flank of Twin Sisters Mountain. After passing several great view-points, you'll reach a large landslide—triggered by 2013 floods—1.3 miles from the trailhead. Beyond the landslide the trail switchbacks above treeline, then twists through bare talus. Marmots and pikas whistle and chirp as dramatic views of Estes Park unfold below. A saddle near the summit is a good place to catch your breath before the final push to either of the two craggy peaks. No matter which you choose, you'll be rewarded with panoramic views stretching from the eastern plains to the rugged Rockies.

TRAILHEAD (Elevation: 9,090') Across the road from Lily Lake, a dirt road heads 0.4 miles uphill to the trailhead. Park on the right side of the road.

TRAIL INFO

RATING Moderate

HIKING TIME 5–6 hours

DISTANCE 7.4 miles, round-trip

ELEVATION CHANGE 2,338 feet

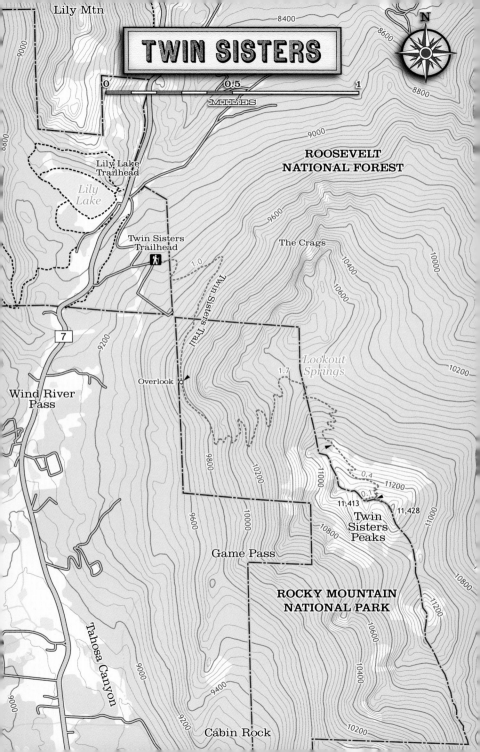

Descending the north slope of Twin Sisters

⊸ OUZEL FALLS ⊱

SUMMARY Ouzel Falls is the most dramatic waterfall in Wild Basin, and the hike there travels through lovely forest and past gorgeous cascades. The hike is particularly striking in early summer, when rivers swell with snowmelt and beautiful wildflowers bloom. From the trailhead follow Wild Basin Trail 0.3 miles to Copeland Falls, which makes a nice, quick detour. The trail continues through shady forest and ascends stone steps, skirting the banks of North Saint Vrain Creek. The creek's bubbling rhythms reach their crescendo at Calypso Cascades (1.8 miles), named after *Calypso bulbosa*, the pink fairy slipper orchid, which grows nearby. Dozens of mini-waterfalls tumble down Cony Creek under three wooden footbridges. Continue 0.9 miles to a wooden footbridge near the waterfall. Ouzel Falls takes its name from Ouzel Creek, which was named by Eno Mills. Ouzels (aka American dippers) are aquatic songbirds that sometimes nest behind waterfalls (p.91).

TRAILHEAD (Elevation: 8,500') Wild Basin Trailhead is located next to the Wild Basin Parking Area.

TRAIL INFO	
RATING Moderate	**DISTANCE** 5.4 miles, round-trip
HIKING TIME 4 hours	**ELEVATION CHANGE** 887 feet

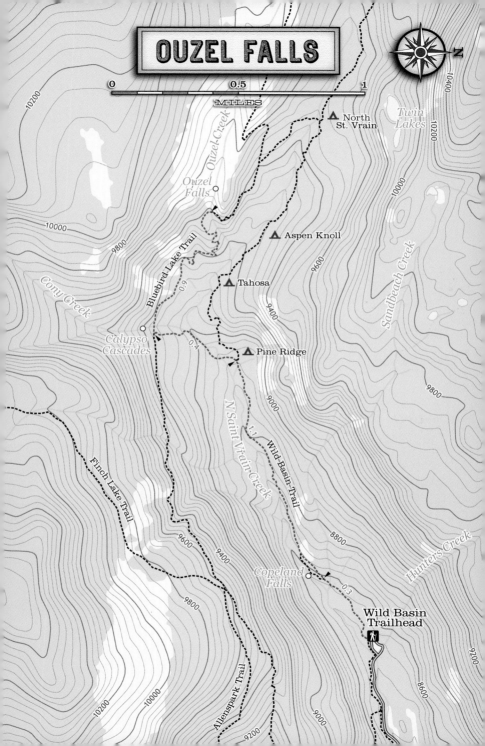

Fairy Slipper
(*Calypso bulbosa*)

Calypso Cascades

⤳ SANDBEACH LAKE ⤳

SUMMARY Want to spend a day at the beach? Perched over 10,000 feet above sea level, this beautiful lake lives up to its name. Its northern shore boasts a pristine sandy beach dotted with evergreens and surrounded by rocky peaks. On a hot summer day there's no better place to cool off and relax. From Sandbeach Lake Trailhead you'll ascend Copeland Moraine, a glacially formed ridge with nice views of North Saint Vrain Creek twisting through Wild Basin below. After veering away from the ridge, the trail steadily ascends through shady forest, crossing Campers Creek and Hunters Creek on narrow wooden footbridges. A final push brings you to the lake's sandy shore. Set back from the beach is a wilderness campsite for backpackers. In the early 1900s, the lake was dammed, creating a reservoir for the nearby town of Longmont. The National Park Service removed the dam in 1988, and falling water levels revealed the sandy beach.

TRAILHEAD (Elevation: 8,345 feet) The Sandbeach Lake Trail starts from the parking area adjacent to the Wild Basin Entrance Station.

TRAIL INFO

RATING Strenuous

HIKING TIME 6 hours

DISTANCE 8.7 miles, round-trip

ELEVATION CHANGE 1,938 feet

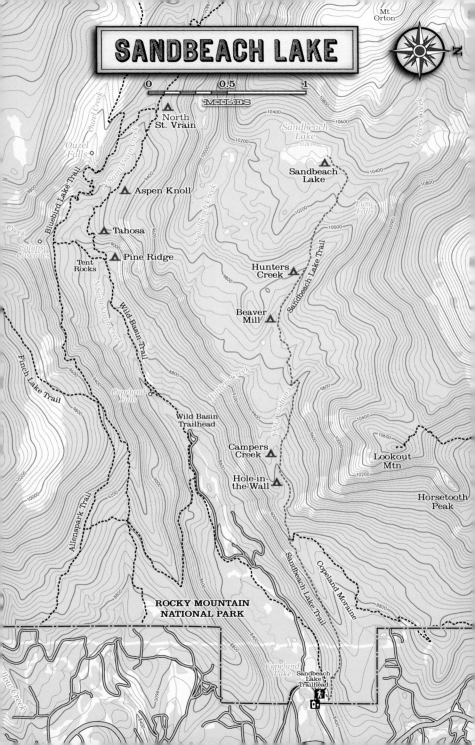

❧ CHASM LAKE ❧

SUMMARY If you're not up for a grueling 15-hour ascent of Longs Peak, Chasm Lake is the next best thing. Rather than stare down from Longs' summit, you'll stare *up* at Longs' summit from the shore of Chasm Lake, situated dramatically below the iconic peak's sheer eastern face. The trail is best in summer and fall, after lingering winter ice and snow have melted, but Chasm Lake is also magnificent when frozen. From Longs Peak Trailhead, the first 3.3 miles follow East Longs Peak Trail, ascending through deep forest and crossing lovely streams before rising above treeline. Roughly 2,100 feet above the trailhead, you'll reach Chasm Junction. Bear left and follow the narrow trail with steep dropoffs, enjoying dramatic views of Peacock Pool and Columbine Falls below. At Chasm Meadows you'll encounter the trail's most formidable challenge: a steep scramble up broken rocks marked by cairns. Once past this final obstacle, you'll stand on the eastern shore of Chasm Lake with Longs Peak towering 2,500 feet above.

TRAILHEAD (Elevation: 9,400') Longs Peak Trailhead is located just past the Longs Peak entrance, 8.5 miles south of Estes Park off Highway 7.

TRAIL INFO

RATING Strenuous   **DISTANCE** 8.5 miles, round-trip

HIKING TIME 6–7 hours   **ELEVATION CHANGE** 2,406 feet

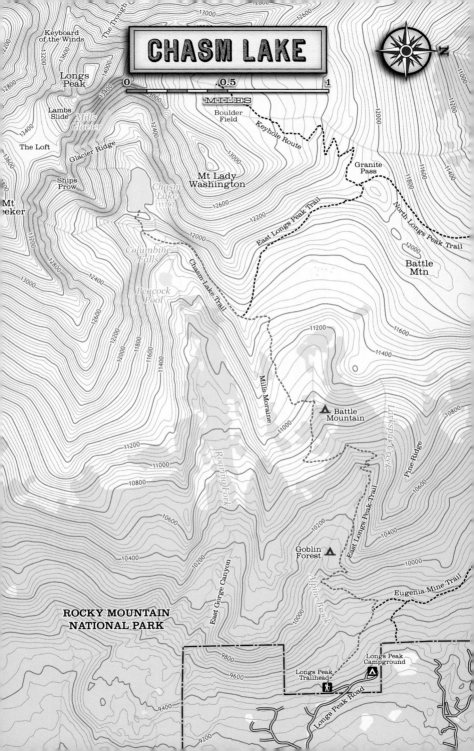

⊰ LONGS PEAK ⊱

SUMMARY The highest peak in Rocky Mountain National Park is one of Colorado's most famous, challenging, and rewarding adventures. Towering 14,259 feet above sea level, Longs Peak isn't just the tallest peak in the park—it's Colorado's northernmost fourteener. The journey to the summit is grueling. From the trailhead you'll rise nearly 4,000 feet to The Keyhole, a dramatic notch in the mountain's northwest flank. Beyond The Keyhole things really get interesting. If hurricane-force winds aren't blowing, you'll spend several hours scrambling over narrow, rugged ledges with terrifying dropoffs. Far more than a hike, Longs Peak is a "nontechnical climb"—and most years the nontechnical climbing season only lasts from July through September. If you've got the physical and mental stamina to make it to the summit, however, you'll be rewarded with some of the best views in the Rockies. A detailed description of climbing Longs Peak is presented on the following pages.

TRAILHEAD (Elevation: 9,400') Longs Peak Trailhead is located just past the Longs Peak entrance station, 8.5 miles south of Estes Park off Highway 7.

◤ TRAIL INFO ◢

RATING Strenuous	**DISTANCE** 14.1 miles, round-trip
HIKING TIME 10–15 hours	**ELEVATION CHANGE** 4,859 feet

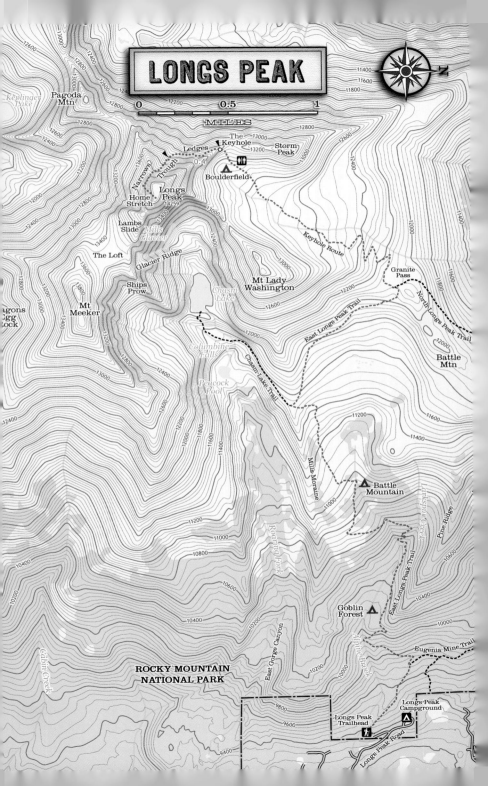

Longs Peak History

The tallest peak in Rocky Mountain National Park is the 15th highest peak in Colorado (and just 172 feet shy of the highest, Mt. Elbert). But few fourteeners have such a colorful history. Its commanding position along the Front Range—visible 100 miles across the eastern plains—has beckoned people for thousands of years. Viewed from the east, Longs Peak forms a twin peak with adjacent Mount Meeker (13,911 feet). The Arapaho call these mountains *nesótaieux*, "The Two Guides," and hunters supposedly climbed Longs Peak to trap eagles for feathers.

STEPHEN LONG

When French trappers arrived in the 1800s, they called the twin mountains *Les Deux Oreilles* ("The Two Ears"). The name Longs Peak was bestowed after the 1819 Yellowstone Expedition led by Major Stephen Harriman Long. On the morning of June 30, 1820, the expedition became the first group of white Americans to formally record the existence of the mountain. Artist Samuel Seymor created the first-ever painting of the Rocky Mountains, which included the summit that would later bear Long's name.

A handful of adventurers claimed to have summitted Longs Peak in the 1860s, but the first successful attempt is officially credited to John Wesley Powell. The Illinois college professor and one-armed Civil War veteran scaled Pikes Peak in 1867, and the following year he returned to conquer Longs Peak. Six men accompanied Powell, including William Byers, editor of the *Rocky Mountain News*. Starting from Grand Lake, the group attempted to summit via Pagoda Mountain, but the harrowing route was too hard. While descending they spotted a gully on the south face, and a man named Lewis Keplinger scouted a plausible route. The next day, August 23, 1868, the group ascended the gully to the top of Longs Peak. Powell congratulated the men, then told them that even greater achievements lay ahead. The following year Powell led the first river expedition through Grand Canyon—an adventure that brought him international fame.

In 1871, three years after Powell's ascent, Addie Alexander and Henrietta Goss became the first women to summit Longs Peak. Later that year itinerant preacher Elkanah Lamb reached The Keyhole with some companions who refused to go any farther. "We have got to climb higher than this if we [want to] get to heaven," Lamb joked. He then summitted alone, feasted "my mental and spiritual and somewhat poetical nature," and descended a treacherous snow gully (now named Lambs Slide) on the sheer eastern face. Lamb eventually settled nearby and became Longs Peak's first climbing guide.

In 1873 the *Rocky Mountain News* chronicled the ascent of Anna Dickenson, a prominent abolitionist and women's rights champion. Later that year Rocky

Mountain Jim hauled English writer Isabella Bird (p.119) to the top of Longs Peak. Their adventure, chronicled in Bird's memoir, *A Lady's Life in the Rocky Mountains*, added yet another chapter to the mountain's growing fame.

Ambitious climbers soon blazed even more challenging routes, and in 1924 Agnes Vaille and Walter Kiener set their stights on the first winter ascent of Longs Peak's rugged east slope. Both Vaille and Kiener were experienced climbers, but multiple failed attempts led Vaille to grow increasingly obsessed with the route. The pair attempted the climb again on January 10, 1925. After a late morning start they did not reach the summit until 4am. Vaille was exhausted and frostbitten, the temperature was 14 degrees below zero, and weather conditions were growing worse. After descending partway, Kiener left Vaille in the shelter of a boulder, then continued on his own. By the time a search party returned, Vaille had frozen to death. Her family later donated funds to construct the Agnes Vaille Memorial Shelter—a stone shelter with a fireplace, wood, and food near the entrance to The Keyhole.

JOHN WESLEY POWELL

Agnes Vaille's cousin, Roger Toll, was superintendent of Rocky Mountain National Park, and following her death he spearheaded the construction of the Boulderfield Hotel. The one-room wooden cabin, located near present-day Boulderfield Campground, boasted a telephone line and was considered the highest hotel in the world. It welcomed guests from 1927 to 1935, but logistical challenges eventually forced it to close.

When big wall rock climbing became popular in the mid-20th century, ambitious rock climbers set their sights on the Diamond, the sheer, 18-acre eastern face of Longs Peak. The National Park Service denied access until 1960, when David Rearick and Robert Kamps conquered the Diamond in 52 hours. In 1990, Estes Park native Tommy Caldwell became the youngest person to climb the Diamond at age 12—a record smashed by 9-year-old Stella Nobel in 2009. Caldwell and Beth Rodden made the first 5.13 ascent of the Diamond in 2001, and Caldwell and Joe Mills made the first 5.14 ascent in 2013.

Andy Anderson holds the record for the fastest ascent of Longs Peak (1 hour 56 minutes, 46 seconds), while rescue ranger Jim "Mr. Longs Peak" Detterline holds the record for the most ascents: 428. Enos Mills, the "father of Rocky Mountain National Park" (p.124), climbed Longs Peak nearly 300 times, and early settler Abner Sprague summitted at age 74.

Longs Peak is the deadliest fourteener in Colorado, claiming over 70 lives since Powell's ascent. But the mountain's high death toll is mostly a reflection of its popularity. These days, roughly 15,000 people reach the summit each year.

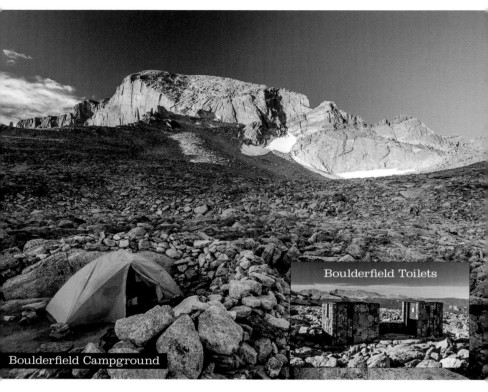

Boulderfield Toilets

Boulderfield Campground

Longs Peak Basics

WEATHER

Longs Peak climbers often start between 1 and 3am to summit and descend before afternoon thunderstorms arrive. Thunderstorms are most common during monsoon season (July, August), but they can happen anytime. If you see dark clouds on the horizon, do not attempt a summit. Late August and early September is considered the best time to climb Longs Peak due to relatively warm temperatures, limited snow, and a high-pressure system that often limits storms. Even if skies are clear, powerful winds can disrupt your plans. The jet stream occasionally dips down and skims the summit of Long Peak, bringing winds that can top 200 mph. For a good weather forecast visit weather.gov and search "Longs Peak."

CAMPING

Camping lets you climb Longs Peak over two days. The best wilderness campground is Boulderfield, located just below The Keyhole. Other campgrounds include Battle Mountain (3.3 miles from The Keyhole), Goblins Forest (4.6 miles from The Keyhole), and Boulder Brook (4.5 miles from The Keyhole). Permits are required for all wilderness campsites (p.20). Longs Peak Campground (p.38) offers car camping near Longs Peak Trailhead.

The Keyhole

GEAR

Summer climbers often wear shorts and T-shirts, but you should always pack a rain jacket, hat, and warm layers. Past the Keyhole you'll do lots of rock scrambling, so I prefer hiking pants, a long-sleeve shirt, and sturdy gloves. Water, food, sunglasses, sunscreen, and a headlamp are essential. A helmet not only protects you from falling rocks, it could save your life after a bad fall.

GUIDED TRIPS

Several local outfitters offer guided ascents. As of this writing outfitters include Kirks Mountain Adventures (kirksmountainadventures.com), Colorado Mountain School (coloradomountainschool.com), and Apexex (apexex.com).

Longs Peak Trail Description

THE KEYHOLE

From Longs Peak Trailhead, follow East Longs Peak Trail towards Chasm Lake (p.194). At Chasm Lake Junction you'll enjoy impressive views of Longs Peak. Bear right and ascend through a dramatic stretch of alpine tundra. As the trail twists higher, you'll enjoy panoramic views stretching from the eastern plains to the Continental Divide. Eventually alpine tundra gives way to the rocky Boulder

The Ledges

Field, which, true to its name, is a massive field of boulders. A well-worn path heads towards two rectangular pit toilets, which mark Boulderfield Campground (elevation 12,700 feet). The award-winning toilets, designed by students from the Colorado Building Workshop using technology from ToiletTech, were installed in 2018 and have revolutionized wilderness waste management. A short distance above the toilets are nine campsites surrounded by protective rock rings. Melting snow feeds small creeks below the rocks, sometimes providing a water source. Beyond the campground, cairns mark the easiest route to The Keyhole, a dramatic notch in the rocks west of the campground. As you approach The Keyhole, be prepared for wobbly rocks underfoot. Adjacent to The Keyhole is a conical stone shelter—a monument to Agnes Vaille, who died attempting a winter summit in 1925. On particularly windy days, when gusts roar through The Keyhole, this is as far as most hikers make it.

THE LEDGES

Upon passing through The Keyhole, you're transported to a new world of rugged terrain unlike anything experienced thus far. Spread out 3,000 feet below is Glacier Gorge, a rocky landscape dotted with alpine lakes. The route to Longs Peak follows the steep cliff to your left. The section, appropriately called the Ledges, is marked by yellow and red bullseyes painted onto rocks. You'll imme-

The Trough

diately get a sense of what's in store for the remainder of the climb: narrow ledges, slippery rocks polished smooth by hiking boots, and sheer drop-offs. Hands and feet are often required to safely navigate the trail. If you don't feel comfortable here, consider turning around. The remaining 1.5 miles to the summit (which can take 2–3 hours) only gets harder. If, on the other hand, you feel comfortable on the Ledges, you can probably handle the rest of the route.

THE TROUGH

After scrambling 0.4 mostly horizontal miles across the Ledges, you'll reach the Trough. This sheltered gully provides some relief from scary dropoffs, but it's a demanding thousand-foot ascent filled with seemingly endless switchbacks. Loose rocks add yet another level of difficulty. The Trough is often covered in deep shadows, and after heavy winters it can retain snow until July or later. (When filled with snow, an ice axe is recommended.) Near the top of the Trough, you'll encounter this section's most formidable obstacle: a 15-foot, Class 3+ technical scramble. Small handholds and footholds help climbers reach the top. Some basic rock climbing experience is helpful. If you're feeling unsure about this short climb, don't hesitate to ask others for assistance. Past the top of the scramble you'll round a corner and encounter the next heart-pounding section: the Narrows.

The Narrows

THE NARROWS

Most hikers experience a jolt of adrenaline upon reaching the Narrows. A vast panorama of Front Range scenery unfolds to the south—stretching 100 miles to Pikes Peak on clear days—while dead ahead the trail clings precipitously to the sheer southern face of Longs Peak. The Narrows is similar to the Ledges, but the route is narrower, the scramble more rugged, and the dropoffs more severe. Take a deep breath and continue ahead. Hands and feet are required along much of the route, and there's no shame in occasionally using your backside. Two-way traffic is difficult along much of the Narrows, and bottlenecks are common. Be prepared for frequent pauses to allow other climbers to pass.

THE HOMESTRETCH

At the end of the Narrows lies the Homestretch—the final push before reaching the summit. Rising nearly 500 vertical feet, the Homestretch is similar to the Trough but steeper and more challenging. This is a serious scramble up smooth granite slabs, and it often requires the use of multiple body parts. Take the time to find solid handholds and footholds, ensuring steady balance throughout your ascent. As with The Narrows, there's no shame in using your backside. Yellow and red bulls eyes guide climbers to the summit.

The Homestretch

THE SUMMIT

Standing on the summit of Longs Peak—the highest point between central Colorado and the North Pole—it feels like all of Colorado is spread out below. On clear days hundred-mile views unfold in all directions—from the eastern plains to Pikes Peak piercing the southern horizon, then west towards the center of the Rockies, all the way north to Wyoming. Loose rocks cover the flat, multi-acre summit, which offers plenty of space to spread out. Most hikers congregate near the highest point on the eastern ledge. After signing the summit register, peer over the ledge, which plummets 2,500 feet to Chasm Lake. If you're looking for peace and solitude, head to the northwest corner to enjoy great views deep into the heart of Rocky Mountain National Park.

In good weather you'll be tempted to linger on the summit for hours. If you see any dark clouds on the horizon, however, you should descend immediately. Storms can arrive with astonishing speed—even on relatively clear days—and lightning strikes have killed hikers. When it's time to leave, head back to the small notch at the top of the Homestretch. Take one last look around, then begin the long journey home. Remember: Most accidents occur on the descent, when people are physically and mentally tired. Sharpen your senses and prepare for an equally thrilling return.

Pikes
Peak

View south from Longs Peak

"Serrated ridges, not much lower than that on which we stood, rose, one beyond another, far as that pure atmosphere could carry the vision, broken into awful chasms deep with ice and snow, rising into pinnacles piercing the heavenly blue with their cold, barren grey, on, on for ever, till the most distant range upbore unsullied snow alone."

—Isabella Bird

"It was something at last to stand upon the storm-rent crown of this lonely sentinel of the Rocky Range, on one of the mightiest of the vertebrae of the backbone of the North American continent, and to see the waters start for both oceans. Uplifted above love and hate and storms of passion, calm amidst the eternal silences, fanned by zephyrs and bathed in living blue, peace rested for that one bright day on the Peak."

—Isabella Bird

Mummy Range

The Boulderfield

View north from Longs Peak

Lumpy
Ridge

Estes
Park

LUMPY RIDGE

THIS DRAMATIC RIDGE rises 1,000 feet above the northern end of Estes Park and marks the eastern boundary of Rocky Mountain National Park. Its unique topography features rounded granite domes that seem to bubble above the evergreens, creating a landscape more evocative of Yosemite or Joshua Tree than the Rockies. Although not nearly as famous as other parts of the park, Lumpy Ridge has plenty of outdoor charm.

Most fascinating is the region's geology. The granite domes that define Lumpy Ridge formed 1.4 billion years ago—300 million years later than most of the park's rocks. Giant plumes of magma rose under the older rocks, then cooled into granite. As erosion removed overlying rocks, pressure on the granite diminished, causing it to expand and crack in concentric layers. When erosion exposed the granite, the concentric layers flaked off like layers of an onion, forming the rounded "exfoliation domes" you see today.

When the Arapaho arrived they named these unusual rocks *nisíthii-bah áh thá*—"Lumpy Ridge." Today the famous lumps are popular with rock climbers, who appreciate both the strength of the granite and its challenging cracks. All routes are trad climbing (rock climbing with non-destructive, removable gear), and there are several great multi-pitch climbs. Be aware that each year some parts of Lumpy Ridge are closed to rock climbing, normally from February 15 through July 31, to protect nesting raptors. Peregrine falcons, prairie falcons, goshawks, red-tailed hawks, and Cooper's hawks are just some of the birds that may be found here. In fact, Lumpy Ridge has the highest concentration of birds of prey in the park.

Lumpy Ridge also boasts several great hikes located a short distance from downtown Estes Park. The highlight is Gem Lake, a jewel-like body of water perched 1,000 feet above Lumpy Ridge Trailhead. An easier option is the short loop hike past Twin Owls.

◀ **BEST HIKES** ▶

TWIN OWLS 214   **GEM LAKE** 216

MacGregor Ranch

This private ranch, located near the base of Lumpy Ridge, was founded in 1873 by Alexander and Clara MacGregor. The ranch has been exquisitely preserved, and today it offers a fascinating window into 19th-century pioneer life. Over two dozen structures are listed on the National Register of Historic Places. From June through August, visitors can enter for a small fee. Guided museum tours focus on the history of homesteading, while self-guided barn tours showcase pre-industrial farming and ranching practices. MacGregor Ranch also offers Heritage Camp, a four-day, hands-on educational program for kids that focuses on homesteading, ranching, and local history. MacGregor Ranch is located 1.5 miles north of Estes Park on MacGregor Ave. (macgregorranch.org, 970-586-3749).

⊰ TWIN OWLS ⊱

SUMMARY This easy loop skirts the southern edge of Lumpy Ridge and passes under Twin Owls, the region's most famous landmark. Viewed from Estes Park, these zoomorphic rock outcrops really do look like a pair of owls keeping a watchful eye over the peaceful valley below. The best views of Twin Owls are from downtown Estes Park, but this hike lets you examine the owls from below. From Lumpy Ridge Trailhead, bear left, pass through a metal gate, and then follow Lumpy Ridge Trail as it twists and turns between fabulous rock outcrops. After 0.6 miles you'll reach an intersection with Black Canyon Trail. Turn right and follow Black Canyon Trail east. As you hike along the trail you'll enjoy glimpses of the rounded tops of the Twin Owls looming high above. After 0.5 miles you'll arrive at a junction with Gem Lake Trail. Turn right to head back to the Lumpy Ridge parking area.

TRAILHEAD (Elevation: 7,840') Lumpy Ridge Trailhead is located at the end of Lumpy Ridge Road, which turns north off Devils Gulch Road. From downtown Estes Park, head north on MacGregor Ave., which turns into Devils Gulch Road.

⊰ TRAIL INFO ⊱

RATING Easy

DISTANCE 1.5 miles, round-trip

HIKING TIME 1 hour

ELEVATION CHANGE 10 feet

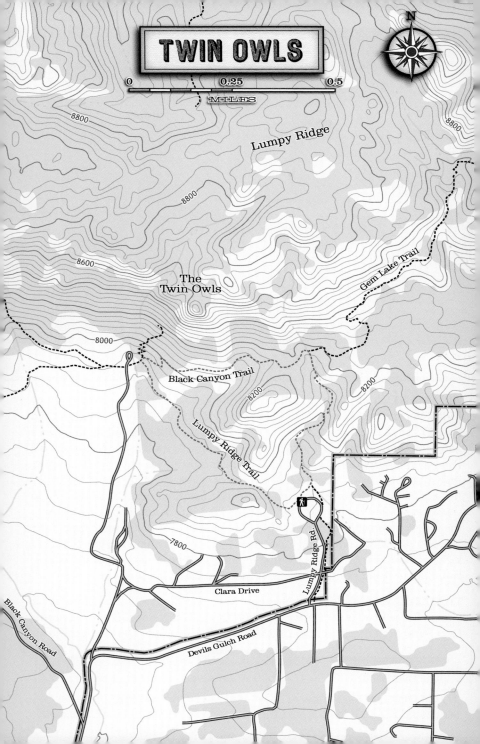

❧ GEM LAKE ❧

SUMMARY Nestled in a rocky bowl high above Estes Park, Gem Lake is Lumpy Ridge's most enchanting destination. From Lumpy Ridge Trailhead, follow Gem Lake Trail as it twists through the surrounding hills. In spring and summer, wildflowers abound. In autumn, golden aspen light up the trail. After 0.5 miles you'll reach a junction with Black Canyon Trail. Bear right and ascend through increasingly dramatic rock formations. Be sure to occasionally turn around and enjoy the expansive views of Estes Park sprawled below the Front Range. Also keep your eyes out for Paul Bunyan's Boot, a boot-shaped rock formation with a hole in the sole. A pit toilet lies off the main trail just before the final push to Gem Lake. There's a sandy beach on Gem Lake's northwest shore, which is a great place to kick back and relax. If you're looking for an even longer hike, continue roughly two miles to Balanced Rock, which delivers exactly what it promises.

TRAILHEAD (Elevation: 7,840') Lumpy Ridge Trailhead is located at the end of Lumpy Ridge Road, which turns north off Devils Gulch Road. From downtown Estes Park, head north on MacGregor Ave, which turns into Devils Gulch Road.

◆ TRAIL INFO ◆

RATING Moderate

HIKING TIME 2.5 hours

DISTANCE 3.5 miles, round-trip

ELEVATION CHANGE 1,004 feet

FALL RIVER

TUMBLING DOWN FROM a glacial cirque below Alpine Visitor Center, Fall River carves a dramatic canyon between Sundance Mountain and the Mummy Range, then gracefully twists through a series of beautiful meadows before exiting the park. Starting from Fall River Entrance, you can trace Fall River to its source, passing wildlife hotspots, dramatic waterfalls, fabulous hiking trails, and panoramic viewpoints along the way.

The adventure begins on Fall River Road, which heads northwest from Estes Park to Fall River Entrance. Continue past Sheep Lakes, turn right on Endovalley Road, and continue to the entrance of Old Fall River Road. From roughly July through September (the exact timing depends on winter snowfall), this one-way dirt road is open to motor vehicles. Rising more than 3,000 feet over 11 miles, Old Fall River Road hugs the southern flank of the Mummy Range above Fall River Valley. After passing a series of steep dropoffs and hairpin turns, the road finishes its rugged journey at Alpine Visitor Center, then connects with Trail Ridge Road.

Before Trail Ridge Road opened in 1932, Old Fall River Road was the only motor route across Rocky Mountain National Park. Prison laborers began construction in 1913, but work paused due to World War I. On September 14, 1920, Fall River Road opened to great fanfare. Stretching from Horseshoe Park to Grand Lake, the new motor road attracted thousands of tourists. Visitors could now travel from Denver to Estes Park, cross the Continental Divide, and loop back to Denver in just three days. The name *Old* Fall River Road was bestowed after the lower reaches of Fall River Road were paved.

Old Fall River Road is distinctly different from Trail Ridge Road. The views aren't as dramatic, and the bumpy dirt road has a speed limit of just 15 mph. But Old Fall River Road reveals a beautiful part of the park filled with hidden gems. If you're looking for an adventure beyond the famous highlights, this rugged road should be near the top of your list.

BEST HIKES

Fall River Visitor Center

This charming visitor center lies five miles west of Estes Park (a quarter-mile east of Fall River Entrance) on Highway 34 / Fall River Road. As you're heading west towards the park, look for the large "Gateway" sign on the left side of the road. The Fall River Visitor Center occupies the left side of the large log-and-stone building. Inside you'll find a staffed help desk, full-size wildlife displays, and a great store run by the nonprofit Rocky Mountain Conservancy. Outside you'll enjoy views of Deer Mountain to the south, MacGregor Mountain to the north, and Fall River running through the valley below. Elk, deer, and bighorn sheep all frequent the surrounding area.

A covered walkway connects Fall River Visitor Center to Rocky Mountain Gateway Store, which sells a vast selection of Rocky Mountain-inspired gifts. Next to the store is Trailhead Restaurant, which serves breakfasts, burgers, sandwiches, and wraps. Adjacent to the building is a small grocery story that sells ice cream and milkshakes.

Also nearby is National Park Gateway Stables, which offers 2-hour horseback rides to Little Horseshoe Park, 4-hour rides to Endovalley, 6-hour rides to the top of Deer Mountain (p.142), and 9-hour rides to Ypsilon Lake (p.234). They also offer 10–30 minute pony rides for "li'l cowpokes" (kids).

Visit rockymountaingateway.net for more information about the restaurant, store, and stables.

Sheep Lakes

This wildlife hotspot, located two miles west of Fall River Entrance, is named after bighorn sheep, which visit these watering holes to indulge in minerals like sodium, iron, magnesium, and zinc. Bighorns deplete essential minerals over long winters, so they visit this natural salt lick to recharge their supplies. Pregnancy and lambing take a significant toll on mineral levels, and bighorn mothers often visit with lambs in late spring. Elk, deer, and moose also visit Sheep Lakes. Wildlife visit throughout the day, but I've had good luck in the early morning. In summer, Sheep Lakes Information Station, located in the parking area, is a good resource for recent sightings and other information.

Wildlife is the main attraction at Sheep Lakes, but these watering holes also have a fascinating geologic history. During the Ice Age a vast glacier flowed down Fall River Canyon. Around 15,000 years ago, when global temperatures warmed, huge ice chunks broke off the melting glacier and settled in the loose, wet sediments. When the ice chunks eventually melted, their depressions filled with water to form Sheep Lakes.

Fall River Valley

Mount Chapin
12,454'

Mt Chiquita
13,069'

Horseshoe Park

Fall River flows through Horseshoe Park in tight, horseshoe-shaped curves, which is how this lovely meadow got its name. There's a great viewpoint on Fall River Road, 0.5 miles past the junction with Endovalley Road. During the Ice Age, when Fall River Glacier flowed down the mountains, it deposited giant mounds of debris on each side, creating two lateral moraines. The glacier also created a large terminal moraine at the front. When the glacier melted, the moraines trapped water and formed an ancient lake. Eventually the lake dried up, and the flat lake bottom became the flat meadow you see today.

Rising high above the western side of Horseshoe Park are the rugged peaks of the Mummy Range. These mountains are named for their supposed resemblance to a reclining Egyptian mummy—an effect that's heightened by snow. The Arapaho call these mountains *nah ou-báatha* ("White Owls").

Ypsilon
Mountain
13,514'

Fairchild
Mountain
13,502'

Roaring
River
Valley

Alluvial Fan

This former catastrophe is one of the most intriguing stops on Fall River Road. In 1903, a group of Loveland farmers built a 26-foot-high earthen dam at Lawn Lake, creating a reservoir 2,200 feet above Horseshoe Park. Eight decades later, on July 15, 1982, heavy rains flooded Lawn Lake. The dam burst at 6am, sending over 300 million gallons of water racing down Roaring River Valley. The 30-foot wall of water gouged out the riverbank and picked up vast quantities of sand, gravel, and boulders. When the flood reached Horseshoe Park, it spread 364,00 cubic feet of debris across a 42-acre alluvial fan (alluvial fans are named for "alluvium" river sediments). The flood continued four miles to Cascade Dam, which it also destroyed, releasing an additional four million gallons of water. Shortly thereafter, a muddy, six-foot wall of water raced through downtown Estes Park. The slurry of mud and debris barrelled into Lake Estes, where Olympus Dam successfully held back the flood. By the time the waters finally receded, three people had lost their lives: a backpacker camped below the dam and two people taking photos of the flood near Aspenglen Campground.

In the aftermath of Lawn Lake Flood, the park service built a trail through Alluvial Fan, but the trail washed away during another flood in 2013. Today an easy, paved path twists 2,000 feet through Alluvial Fan. A sturdy wooden bridge spans Roaring River, and there's a nice viewpoint near Horseshoe Falls. The best views of Alluvial Fan, which really put Lawn Lake Flood in perspective, are from Rainbow Curve (p.243) on Trail Ridge Road.

10,000-foot view

Endovalley Picnic Area (mile 0)

Old Fall River Road starts at the end of Endovalley Road next to Endovalley Picnic Area. A metal gate marks the entrance to Old Fall River Road, which continues 11 miles to Alpine Visitor Center (p.259). The dirt road loosely follows an old Arapaho trail called *éthebáw*, the "Dog Trail," because Arapaho dogs once pulled travois (wooden sleds) up the trail.

Chasm Falls (mile 1.4)

This beautiful waterfall is one of the highlights of Old Fall River Road. Just above the waterfall there's a small parking area with a paved trail that descends to a protected viewpoint. From there you'll enjoy dramatic views of the 25-foot waterfall as it tumbles through a narrow granite chasm. Note: During peak season Chasm Falls parking area quickly fills. Try to visit in early morning or late afternoon.

Gabions (mile 3.8)

In 1953, a massive rockslide caused so much damage to Old Fall River Road that the road was nearly abandoned. In 1967, the park installed rock-filled, wire-mesh cages called gabions (from the Italian *gabbione* "big cage") at the most rockslide-prone areas. The sturdy gabions have held firm ever since. Near the top of the gabions there's a hairpin turn with dramatic views down Fall River Valley. At this point the elevation is roughly 10,000 feet—nearly two miles above sea level.

Chasm Falls

Cañoncito (mile 5.1)

Cañoncito is Spanish for "Little Canyon," which is exactly what you'll find about halfway up Old Fall River Road. During the Ice Age, Fall River Glacier scoured Fall River Valley and scraped away everything but the bedrock, which was polished smooth under the glacier's enormous weight. When the glacier melted roughly 7,500 years ago, Fall River set to work eroding the granite. A few thousand years later the river carved this lovely mini-canyon filled with waterfalls and cascades. Past Cañoncito, Old Fall River Road rises above Fall River.

Fall River Cirque (mile 8)

After rising through several miles of subalpine forest, Old Fall River Road bursts above treeline into a large expanse of alpine tundra. Glorious views unfold in all directions, with Fall River Cirque dominating the western horizon. This enormous basin, which measures three-quarters of a mile across and half a mile deep, was carved by Ice Age glaciers. Around two million years ago, when the Ice Age began, heavy snow compacted into ice, which eventually flowed under the pressure of its own weight and became a glacier. As global temperatures warmed and cooled over the past two million years, multiple glaciers descended from Fall River Cirque. The most recent, Fall River Glacier, stretched nearly nine miles to present-day Fall River Entrance.

Fall River Road curves around a small pond, then enters a section where winter snowdrifts sometimes top 30 feet. This is the most difficult section of road to clear each spring. In the 1920s, park employees grew so frustrated with the snowdrifts they blasted them away with dynamite. The challenges of maintaining Fall River Road ultimately led to the construction of Trail Ridge Road.

Past this final section lies Fall River Pass. Located 11,796 feet above sea level, Fall River Pass divides Fall River Watershed and Cache la Poudre Watershed, both of which drain into the South Platte River. Old Fall River Road finishes its journey at Alpine Visitor Center (p.259), located near the halfway point of Trail Ridge Road. After enjoying spectacular views of Fall River Cirque from the visitor center and adjacent balcony, you can drive east on Trail Ridge Road to Estes Park or west on Trail Ridge Road to Grand Lake.

Alpine Visitor Center

⊰ YPSILON LAKE ⊱

SUMMARY Ypsilon Mountain is one of the Mummy Range's most famous peaks, and this hike takes you to a pretty lake nestled beneath its iconic southeast face. From Lawn Lake Trailhead follow the steep trail as it rises above Horseshoe Park to Roaring River, which was gouged out by floods in 1982 and 2013 (p.227). The trail parallels the river to a junction 1.3 miles past the trailhead. Bear left, cross the log bridge, and begin a 2.4-mile ascent through dense lodgepole pine forest. After cresting at 10,744 feet, the trail drops to Chipmunk Lake, a small pond with great views, then continues 0.4 miles to Ypsilon Lake. Strong, adventurous hikers with good route-finding skills can continue roughly one mile to Spectacle Lakes, a pair of eyeglass-shaped lakes directly below Ypsilon Mountain. If scrambling up steep, wet rock slabs doesn't intimidate you, Spectacle Lakes is a gorgeous destination.

TRAILHEAD (Elevation: 8,540') Lawn Lake Trailhead is located just past the start of Endovalley Road on the right.

TRAIL INFO

RATING Strenuous	**DISTANCE** 8.8 miles, round-trip
HIKING TIME 6 hours	**ELEVATION CHANGE** 2,204 feet

TRAIL RIDGE ROAD

TRAIL RIDGE ROAD is the highest continuous paved road in America and the driving highlight of Rocky Mountain National Park. This 40-mile "Highway to the Sky" climbs over 12,000 feet above sea level. Along the way it passes panoramic viewpoints, skirts plunging canyons, and showcases one of the most dramatic expanses of alpine tundra in Colorado. Although heavy snow closes Trail Ridge Road approximately seven months a year, when open it reveals some of the most inspiring scenery in the Rockies.

You can easily spend a full day exploring Trail Ridge Road. There are nearly a dozen famous viewpoints and several excellent hiking trails. Short hikes include Tundra Communities Trail (p.250), Alpine Ridge Trail (p.259), and Lake Irene (p.266). Those looking for a longer hike can explore the Ute Trail (p.270), which follows an ancient path used by native tribes.

Several outfitters, including the nonprofit Rocky Mountain Conservancy, offer driving tours along Trail Ridge Road (p.36). If you're driving your own vehicle, consider heading up Old Fall River Road (p.219)—a one-way road that merges with Trail Ridge Road—crossing the Continental Divide (p.265), descending to Kawuneeche Valley (p.273), then returning via Trail Ridge Road.

When the first heavy snow falls, often in late October, Trail Ridge Road closes from Many Parks Curve (p.240) to Colorado River Trailhead. It normally reopens in late May/early June, but exact dates depend on winter snowfall. Two plowing crews, starting at opposite ends of Trail Ridge Road, begin clearing snow in mid-April, then meet in the middle.

Two road crews constructed Trail Ridge Road in the early 1930s. One crew worked on the eastern section, the other crew worked on the western section, and by 1932 the new highway across Trail Ridge was completed. Interestingly, the name Tombstone Ridge was once suggested for Trail Ridge. Had that name been chosen, fewer visitors might be enticed to drive on "Tombstone Ridge Road."

BEST HIKES

UTE TRAIL 270 TUNDRA COMMUNITIES TRAIL 250

Beaver Ponds

Beaver Ponds (mile 1.8)

This unmarked stop features a short, elevated boardwalk above small beaver ponds. It's a lovely place to take a quick stroll and look for wildlife. The large ridge just north of Beaver Ponds is a lateral moraine that formed when Fall River Glacier flowed through Horseshoe Park between 25,000 and 10,000 years ago. The moraine separates Horseshoe Park from Hidden Valley, which is the next stop on Trail Ridge Road.

Hidden Valley (mile 2.4)

This peaceful valley—"hidden" from Horseshoe Park by a glacially formed lateral moraine—was once the site of Hidden Valley Ski Area. In the 1930s, trucks shuttled skiers up Trail Ridge Road so they could ski through trees and powder fields to Hidden Valley below. Over the following decades, Hidden Valley added a base lodge, chairlifts, and ski tows above treeline. Skiers enjoyed over 1,200 acres and 2,000 vertical feet of terrain. Although Hidden Valley was loved by locals, operating a small ski resort inside a national park posed many logistical challenges, and the resort closed for good in 1991.

Fortunately, there's still plenty of winter fun. Hidden Valley is great for sledding and tubing, and backcountry skiers enjoy Hidden Valley's "ghost" trails. In summer the park's Junior Ranger Headquarters is located here, and there's an easy, half-mile interpretive trail.

Many Parks Curve (mile 4)

Not long after Trail Ridge Road starts its multi-mile ascent to the "rooftop of America," it passes this sweeping viewpoint (elevation 9,640 feet), which looms high above Horseshoe Park, Little Horseshoe Park, Beaver Meadows, and Moraine Park. In Colorado the word "park" often means meadow—a tradition that comes from French-speaking trappers, who arrived in the 1800s and called mountain meadows "parques."

There are two parking areas at Many Parks Curve. If you're ascending, park at the upper parking area (past the viewpoint) and follow the short walkway down to the viewpoint. If you're descending, park at the lower parking area next to the viewpoint. There's an interesting rock outcrop next to the lower parking area. Scramble up the rocks for a nice view of Horseshoe Park (p.224) to the north. After enjoying the views, look down at your feet. The rocks you're standing on are 1.7 billion years old—nearly half the age of the earth! These

North Lateral Moraine

Lower Beaver Meadows

Upper Beaver Meadows

rocks formed during the uplift of an ancient mountain range that predated the Rockies. The dark rocks are biotite schist—a metamorphic rock that formed when tectonic movement transformed (metamorphosed) previously existing layers of sedimentary rocks through heat and pressure. In places the dark schist is shot through with narrow bands of light granite. Three hundred million years after the schist formed, hot magma flowed into cracks in the schist and cooled into light-colored granite.

The southern view over Moraine Park reveals how Ice Age glaciers sculpted the present landscape. As the Thompson Glacier flowed east down the Front Range, it acted like a massive conveyor belt, transporting rocks and debris to both sides. Those massive debris piles, called lateral moraines, are still there today. A terminal moraine formed at the front of the glacier, and when the glacier melted a large lake settled between the three moraines. The ancient lake bottom slowly filled with sediment and organic debris, and when the lake drained it left behind the beautiful flat meadow you see today.

South Lateral Moraine

Moraine Park

MacGregor
Mountain

Alluvial Fan

Rainbow Curve (mile 8)

Perched over two miles above sea level (10,829 feet), Rainbow Curve offers a fabulous bird's-eye view of Horseshoe Park. Rainbows, while not common, are sometimes seen after summer afternoon thunderstorms. With panoramic views east, this is also Trail Ridge Road's best place to watch sunrise. As you gaze across the scenery, look for Fall River as it carves tight, horseshoe-shaped loops through the meadow 2,300 feet below. On the northwest edge of Horseshoe Park lies Alluvial Fan—the dramatic remains of the catastrophic 1982 and 2013 floods (p.227). Across the meadow is a lateral moraine, which hides Hidden Valley from Horseshoe Park. During the Ice Age, Fall River Glacier flowed nearly nine miles from Alpine Visitor Center across Horseshoe Park, leaving enormous moraines in its wake. Rising above the northeast end of Horseshoe Park are Mount MacGregor and Lumpy Ridge, two large granite masses whose rounded domes are the result of exfoliation. This geologic process occurs when erosion removes overlying rocks along concentric cracks, allowing underlying layers to expand and flake off like layers of an onion, leaving a rounded dome behind.

Lumpy Ridge

terminal moraine

lateral moraine

lateral moraine

Hidden Valley

Longs
Peak

Treeline

Beyond Rainbow Curve, Trail Ridge Road rises above treeline. Before reaching vast expanses of alpine tundra you'll notice small trees twisted and gnarled into unusual shapes. This is the krummholz (p.73), the last outpost of tree life before survival becomes impossible. *Krummholz* is a German word that means "crooked wood." In this rugged transition zone, trees grow stout and twisted due to regular, hurricane-force winds. Look closely, and you'll notice that some trees only have branches on their leeward side (away from prevailing winds). Krummholz trees often cluster together in small "islands" for additional wind protection. White-tailed ptarmigans (p.88), who live in alpine tundra year-round, seek winter shelter in these scattered tree islands. Despite the challenges of living in the krummholz, some trees can live 1,000 years or longer.

Over one-third of Rocky Mountain National Park is located above treeline, which generally occurs between 11,000 and 11,500 feet. Trail Ridge Road boasts roughly 11 miles above treeline. Driving through this region, you'll notice tall, wooden poles planted along the side of the road. These poles are used to mark the edge of the road when spring snowplows arrive. In places Trail Ridge Road snowdrifts can reach 20 feet or higher.

Forest Canyon Overlook (mile 10.9)

After a short drive along Tombstone Ridge—named for its tombstone-like rocks—you'll reach the parking area at Forest Canyon Overlook. A short trail leads to a panoramic viewpoint enclosed by rock walls. You are now standing 11,716 feet above sea level. Directly in front of you, Forest Canyon plummets 2,200 feet, then rises to 12,000-foot peaks along the Continental Divide. Beyond these peaks, rivers and streams flow into the Colorado River en route to the Pacific Ocean.

During the Ice Age, between 25,000 and 15,000 years ago, Forest Canyon filled with ice. Multiple small glaciers flowed down from the surrounding peaks, coalescing into the enormous Thompson Glacier, which was roughly 1,500 feet thick. At its maximum extent, roughly 18,000 years ago, the Thompson Glacier stretched 13 miles to Moraine Park. The tallest peaks lay above the ice, but the bowl-shaped glacial cirque below Terra Tomah Mountain is a classic example of how glaciers carved away at the mountains.

Past Forest Canyon Overlook, Trail Ridge Road wraps around the southern flank of Sundance Mountain, which was named by an old miner who lived near its base. Each morning the miner watched the sun dance across the eastern face of the mountain, so he named it Sundance.

Heyden Spire
12,480'

Heyden
Gorge

Terra Tomah
Mountain
12,718'

Mount Ida
12,880'

Glacial
Cirque

Mount
Julian

Mount
Ida

Rock Cut (mile 12.8)

This section of Trail Ridge Road slices through a blasted-out corridor of ancient rock, exposing a fascinating geologic story. Here, 12,100 feet above sea level, you'll drive through the remnants of a two-billion-year-old sea. As ancient rivers flowed into the sea, they deposited thick layers of clay, silt, and sand, which eventually compressed into shale, siltstone, and sandstone. A few hundred million years later, tectonic forces pushed these sedimentary rocks into a giant mountain range, subjecting them to enormous heat and pressure. The shale metamorphosed into schist, while siltstone and sandstone metamorphosed into gneiss. In places light bands cut across the darker metamorphic rocks, revealing areas where magma flowed into cracks in the rocks. When the magma cooled, it solidified into light-colored granite and pegmatite.

After driving west through Rock Cut, park on the right side of the road. Walk across Trail Ridge Road and peer over the stone guardrail. Throughout summer the ridge below is a popular gathering spot for elk and bighorn sheep (p.92). If you don't see either of those animals, listen for the playful chirps of marmots and pikas (p.101). Directly across Forest Canyon lies Mt. Ida, which rises above a string of six alpine lakes called Gorge Lakes. In the Swiss and Italian Alps such stairstep lakes are called *pater noster* ("our father" in Latin) because they resemble a string of rosary beads. There's no trail to Gorge Lakes. Only the most rugged backpackers have visited these pristine lakes, where the Arapaho once hunted bear and other animals.

Tundra Communities Trail

Just west of Rock Cut lies one of the highlights of Trail Ridge Road: Tundra Communities Trail. This half-mile paved trail rises 260 feet through alpine tundra, revealing some of the most interesting scenery in the park. The trail is relatively easy, but it's located over 12,000 feet above sea level, so low oxygen levels can challenge some hikers. Also keep an eye out for dark clouds, which can signal an approaching lightning storm.

To the right of the trailhead is a small, fenced-off plot. In 1958, alpine botanist Beatrice Willard established this research site, which she carefully monitored for decades. Willard co-authored the 1972 nature classic *The Land Above The Trees*, and in 2007 her research site became the first-ever ecological research plot added to the National Register of Historic Places.

Tundra Communities Trail rises quickly from the parking area before gradually flattening out. Always stay on the paved trail. Alpine tundra is fragile, and even mild disturbances can take decades to heal. At the end of the trail is a rock outcrop. Nimble hikers can scramble up the rocks, where panoramic views and a metal peak finder await.

Alpine Tundra

The rugged landscape above treeline is home to one of earth's most remarkable ecosystems: alpine tundra (p.74). The word *tundra*, which comes from the Sámi people of Scandinavia and Russia, means "land of no trees." Vast expanses of arctic tundra grow near sea level in the northernmost reaches of Russia, Scandinavia, Alaska, and Canada. Below Canada, however, tundra only exists at the highest elevations. Rocky Mountain National Park protects the largest expanse of alpine tundra in the lower 48 states, offering visitors a fascinating glimpse of this unique landscape. Between June and August, over 100 species of flowering plants bloom in Rocky's alpine tundra. During this time elk and bighorn sheep migrate above treeline to feast on the vast natural bounty. This, in turn, attracted native tribes, who climbed above treeline to hunt. Remnants of "game drives," long stone walls used to funnel prey towards concealed hunters (p.106), are scattered throughout the park's alpine tundra. Over 50 game drives have been discovered nearby—more than anywhere in Colorado.

Lava Cliffs (mile 15)

Past Rock Cut, Trail Ridge Road twists through a gently rolling landscape. Such landscapes are often indicators of Ice Age glaciers, but this terrain largely pre-dates the Ice Age. Before glaciers descended from the highest elevations, the Rocky Mountains consisted of gently rounded mountaintops interlaced with V-shaped valleys carved by rivers. When global temperatures dropped, glaciers flowed down the V-shaped valleys and sculpted them into enormous U-shaped valleys. The highest peaks remained above the glaciers, however, and today some of the park's highest elevations, including this section of Trail Ridge Road, are the smooth remnants of ancient mountaintops.

At mile 15, 12,000 feet above sea level, there's a pullout for Lava Cliffs. These stark, reddish cliffs consist of ash-flow rhyolite tuffs, which is a fancy way of saying they came from volcanos. Starting around 29 million years ago, volcanoes

Specimen Mountain
12,489 feet

erupted eight miles west in the Never Summer Mountains. The eruptions lasted five million years and spewed vast quantities of red-hot ash across the landscape. The volcanic ash—a mixture of feldspar, quartz, and molten rock—cooled and solidified into rock, which was later exposed by Ice Age glaciers. Iceberg Lake, nestled in the glacial cirque below Lava Cliffs, is named for small "icebergs" that sometimes break off the surrounding snowbanks and drift into the lake.

Three miles northwest lies Specimen Mountain. Geologists once thought Specimen Mountain was a volcano, but recent studies have concluded otherwise. Interestingly, the Arapaho name for Specimen Mountain is "Mountain Smokes," and oral histories tell of the mountain roaring, rumbling, and spewing hot rocks.

A short distance past Lava Cliffs, Trail Ridge Road reaches its highest elevation: 12,183 feet. There are no pullouts or parking areas to enjoy this milestone, so continue driving to Gore Range Overlook.

Forest
Canyon
Pass

Gore Range Overlook (mile 16)

Beyond Lava Cliffs, dramatic views unfold to the west, and 12,010-foot Gore Range Overlook is a great place to enjoy them. The overlook is named for the Gore Range, which on clear days can be seen on the horizon. The mountains are named for Lord St. George Gore, one of Britain's wealthiest men, who invested in cheap real estate following the Irish Potato Famine. Gore visited Colorado on a notorious 1855 hunting expedition that included 40 men and 100 horses. After Gore shot thousands of animals, local tribes, outraged at such waste, asked him to leave, then robbed him as he departed.

Below the overlook lies Forest Canyon Pass, one of the most important native sites in the park, which was used seasonally as both a hunting camp and a sacred vision quest site. The western skyline is dominated by the 12,000-foot peaks of the Never Summer Mountains. The name comes from the Arapaho word *ni-chébe-chii*, "never no summer"—an appropriate description for mountains where snowdrifts often linger year-round. The Continental Divide runs along the crest of the Never Summer Mountains, which includes such fabulously named peaks as Mount Cirrus, Mount Nimbus, and Mount Cumulus.

Alpine Visitor Center (mile 16.9)

Perched 11,796 feet above sea level, this is the highest national park visitor center in America. Alpine Visitor Center opened its doors in 1965 to help celebrate the 50th anniversary of Rocky Mountain National Park. But its extreme location posed some unusual challenges. Winter winds can sometimes top 200 mph, so heavy logs were laid across the roof to protect it from blowing away. The logs also provide structural support against deep, heavy snow.

Alpine Visitor Center is open Memorial Day Weekend through Columbus Day (weather permitting). Inside you'll find picture windows with dramatic views, natural history exhibits, restrooms, and a bookstore run by the Rocky Mountain Conservancy. Next to the visitor center is Trail Ridge Store and the Café at Trail Ridge (trailridgegiftstore.com). This is a great place to relax and enjoy hot chocolate or coffee, especially during bad weather. Be aware that during peak season (July, August, weekends in June and September) the adjacent parking area often fills to capacity between 10am and 3pm.

Alpine Visitor Center is located at Fall River Pass, which divides the watersheds of Fall River and Cache La Poudre River. The visitor center sits on the edge of Fall River Cirque, a three-quarter-mile-wide by half-mile-deep bowl carved by glaciers. For a bird's-eye view of these dramatic surroundings, including panoramic views of distant peaks, climb quarter-mile Alpine Ridge Trail. The trail's concrete steps rise 209 feet above Alpine Visitor Center to a viewpoint 12,005 feet above sea level.

Never Summer
Mountains

Medicine Bow Curve (mile 17.3)

This hairpin turn, located 11,640 feet above sea level, reveals distant views of the Medicine Bow Mountains—a 100-mile mountain range that stretches across the Colorado/Wyoming border. The origin of the name "Medicine Bow" is shrouded in mystery. Some claim the region is home to mountain mahogany native tribes prized for bow-making. When friendly tribes gathered to make bows they discussed medicine, and early white settlers, conflating the two activities, named the region "Medicine Bow."

With sweeping western views, Medicine Bow Curve is a fabulous place to watch sunset. No matter when you visit, you'll enjoy beautiful views of Cache la Poudre River twisting through a narrow meadow below. During the Ice Age, an enormous glacier filled Cache la Poudre Valley to present-day treeline.

Specimen
Mountain
12,489 feet

Cache la Poudre River (below) was
named by French trappers who hid
a stash (*cache*) of gunpowder (*poudre*)
along the river's banks in 1836.

Poudre Lake

Milner Pass (mile 21)

You can see the Continental Divide from many points on Trail Ridge Road, but there's only one place where the road actually *crosses* the Continental Divide: 10,759-foot Milner Pass. A large sign next to the parking area marks the exact dividing line. All precipitation that falls left of the sign drains into Cache la Poudre River, which flows into the Platte River, the Missouri River, the Mississippi River, and the Atlantic Ocean—a journey of 2,600 miles. All precipitation that falls right of the sign drains into the Colorado River, which flows 1,500 miles to the Pacific Ocean. The two paths could not be more different. The eastern path is a relatively languid journey across the Great Plains to the Mississippi. The western path tumbles down the Rockies, slices through the desert Southwest, and carves Grand Canyon in the process. These days, however, the Colorado River is so depleted by irrigation that it no longer reaches the sea.

The Arapaho call this place *ba háa-thosōn*, "Deer Pass." Poudre Lake, located next to the pass, is indeed a great place to see deer—as well as elk and moose. The name Milner Pass comes from T.J. Milner, a railroad promoter who surveyed this land but never achieved his dream of laying tracks across the Continental Divide. An easy hiking trail skirts the southern shore of Poudre Lake, then rises to some dramatic rock pillars. These pillars formed 1.7 billion years ago, when magma flowed into cracks in the previously formed metamorphic schist, then cooled into pegmatite. Because pegmatite is harder than schist, the surrounding schist eroded faster, leaving these dramatic pillars behind.

Lake Irene (mile 21.8)

This lovely lake, located three-quarters of a mile past Milner Pass, is a great place to take a leisurely stroll or enjoy a relaxed picnic. An easy 0.8-mile hiking trail loops around Lake Irene, which was named after a guest at "Squeaky Bob" Wheeler's Hotel de Hardscrabble, a nearby dude ranch that hosted visitors in the early 1900s. The trail starts near the picnic area above the lake's northern shore. About halfway down the trail, a short spur trail leads to a pleasant viewpoint above a large meadow.

Farview Curve (mile 23.1)

From this hairpin curve, located 10,120 feet above sea level, you'll enjoy great views of Kawuneeche Valley, which extends along the eastern base of the Never Summer Mountains. During the Ice Age, the largest glacier in Rocky Mountain National Park stretched 20 miles through this valley. At its maximum extent, roughly 20,000 years ago, the glacier was 2,200 feet thick and Farview Curve was buried under 1,000 feet of ice. After the glacier melted, the modern Colorado River flowed through Kawuneeche Valley.

High above the valley, on the eastern slope of Red Mountain, lies a prominent scar. This is Grand Ditch, a 130-year-old water project that catches runoff from the Never Summer Mountains and diverts it to Colorado's thirsty eastern plains. When construction began in 1890, the Colorado River was called the Grand River

(hence the name Grand Ditch), and laborers used picks, shovels, and blasting powder to carve a ditch along the mountainside. Horses and machinery later helped expand the 20-foot-wide channel. By the time Grand Ditch was finished in 1936, it extended 14.3 miles and captured water from a dozen streams, diverting roughly 30% of the total runoff of the Never Summer Mountains. Grand Ditch is privately owned, and it continues to divert 20,000 acre-feet per year across the Continental Divide via Cache la Poudre River.

In 2003, following heavy spring snowmelt, a 100-foot section of Grand Ditch breached its banks, unleashing 50,000 cubic yards of water. The resulting flood destroyed 20,000 trees, damaged wetlands near Lulu City (p.116), and altered the course of the Colorado River. The scar from this breach is still visible today. In 2008 the owners of Grand Ditch paid the National Park Service nine million dollars in damages.

Grand Ditch

◁ UTE TRAIL ▷

SUMMARY This dramatic trail, which follows an ancient path used by the Ute and Arapaho tribes, is one of the highlights of Trail Ridge Road. Skirting the edge of Forest Canyon, the Ute Trail passes through alpine tundra and treats hikers to panoramic 11,000-foot views. To the west lie the rugged peaks above Forest Canyon. The southern horizon is dominated by Longs Peak and the Front Range. After two miles you'll reach Timberline Pass, which offers tremendous eastern views 4,000 feet above Estes Park. The entire six-mile trail descends 3,500 feet from Trail Ridge Road to Upper Beaver Meadows. But hiking two relatively flat miles along Tombstone Ridge to Timberline Pass is an easy option with great rewards. The trail below Timberline Pass is extremely steep. The Arapaho call it *taíeonbää*, "Where the Children Walked," because children would dismount their horses and walk up the difficult path.

TRAILHEAD (Elevation: 11,437') Ute Trailhead is two miles west of Rainbow Curve and one mile east of Forest Canyon Overlook. There's a small parking area next to the trailhead, plus additional parking a short distance west.

TRAIL INFO

RATING Moderate	**DISTANCE** 3.9 miles, round-trip
HIKING TIME 3 hours	**ELEVATION CHANGE** 222 feet

KAWUNEECHE VALLEY

STRETCHING 10 MILES along the western boundary of Rocky Mountain National Park, Kawuneeche Valley showcases the gorgeous scenery west of the Continental Divide. This is the birthplace of the Colorado River, which flows through the center of the valley and nourishes a lush habitat. Although not as dramatic as the bold peaks of the Front Range, or as heartpounding as the scenery along Trail Ridge Road, Kawuneeche Valley has its own laid-back charm. Sadly, parts of the valley burned during the 2020 East Troublesome Fire (p.130), and it will be years before they fully recover.

Fewer than 20 percent of visitors enter Rocky Mountain National Park via Kawuneeche Valley, which means limited crowds even in summer. There are no shuttles, but there are plenty of great hikes. Nestled between the Front Range and the Never Summer Mountains, there's an abundance of beautiful meadows, waterfalls, and alpine lakes. In winter, when the road stays open 10 miles to the Colorado River Trailhead, this is a great place to snowshoe and cross-country ski.

Prior to the arrival of white settlers, the Utes and Arapahoes seasonally visited this area to hunt. The name Kawuneeche comes from the Arapaho word *káh ah wu-ná chee*, which means "Coyote Creek"—their name for the Colorado River. It's possible to see coyotes, but these days the wildlife highlight is moose (p.97), which live here in greater numbers than anywhere else in the park.

South of Kawuneeche Valley lies Grand Lake, the largest natural lake in Colorado, and two large reservoirs: Shadow Mountain Lake and Lake Granby. These three lakes, which lie just outside the park, offer terrific boating and kayaking, and the small towns nearby have some great restaurants and lodges. So you can enjoy the best of both worlds—the rugged beauty of Kawuneeche Valley and modern creature comforts. What's not to love?

BEST HIKES

Holzwarth Historic Site

Pickled in a century-old time warp, this historic lodge offers a fascinating glimpse of rugged pioneer life. Following Colorado's enactment of Prohibition in 1916, Denver saloonkeeper John Holzwarth brought his family to Kawuneeche Valley to homestead a ranch along the Colorado River. The German immigrant realized there was more money in tourism than ranching, so he constructed a trout fishing lodge. His wife, Sophie ("Mama") Holzwarth, cooked local trout, venison, and grouse, which were complimented with ranch-produced chicken, eggs, and milk. The Holzwarths followed in the footsteps of Robert "Squeaky Bob" Wheeler, who established the "Hotel de Hardscrabble" at the north end of Kawuneeche Valley a decade earlier. Wheeler's tent camp was rugged and primitive, but it attracted visitors, including Teddy Roosevelt, who were more interested in natural beauty than creature comforts. Squeaky Bob's was a classic dude ranch—a name derived from cattle-rancher slang for Eastern city-slickers ("dudes") who ventured West on vacation.

In 1973, John Holzwarth, Jr. sold the property to The Nature Conservancy, which sold it to the National Park Service. Today volunteers offer free tours from mid-June through Labor Day. The Holzwarth Historic Site parking area is located 0.5 miles south of Timber Creek Campground (eight miles north of Grand Lake Entrance Station). From the parking area a half-mile, family-friendly trail crosses the Colorado River to the historic buildings.

Colorado River

Born a few miles north of Kawuneeche Valley, the Colorado River begins its epic journey in Rocky Mountain National Park. After gently flowing through Kawuneeche Valley, the river tumbles down the Rockies into the desert Southwest, slicing through the crumbling landscape and carving a series of stunning canyons—most famously Grand Canyon—before flowing towards the Sea of Cortez. Along the way it sustains the most prosperous desert civilization in the world, earning the nickname the "American Nile."

Prior to 1921, however, the river that flows through Kawuneeche Valley was called the Grand River. Back then the Colorado River officially started below the confluence of the Grand River and the Green River near Moab, Utah. To Colorado congressman Edward Taylor it was an "abomination" the Colorado River did not start in his state. He considered Grand River "a meaningless misnomer. Practically everything in Colorado is grand!"—so he petitioned the federal government to change the name. Representatives from Wyoming argued the Green River was longer, and thus the Colorado River's true headwaters began in their state. Taylor countered that the Grand River contributed more water by volume. And so, on July 25, 1921, the Grand River officially became the Colorado River. The river's original name still lingers in places like Grand Lake, Grand Ditch, Grand County, and Grand Junction.

Coyote Valley

This easy, family-friendly trail follows a lovely stretch of the Colorado River past beautiful meadows with mountain views. The trailhead is located two miles south of Holzwarth Historic Site (six miles north of Grand Lake Entrance). The half-mile trail is stroller- and wheelchair-accessible. Picnic tables and wooden benches offer plenty of opportunities to relax and enjoy the scenery. No matter what your hiking ability, Coyote Valley Trail is one of the best ways to experience the peaceful beauty of Kawuneeche Valley.

Little Buckaroo Ranch Barn

It's easy to miss this historic barn, located down a dusty path at the end of an unmarked dirt road. But if you enjoy classic Western scenery, it's worth a visit. Featured in multiple Coors beer commercials, Little Buckaroo Ranch Barn is one of Colorado's most distinctive barns—with arguably the best name. Constructed in 1942, it's actually a Cajun-style barn with a square base, monitor roof, and rustic log slab siding. It was built by a Louisiana couple, Frank and Mary Godchaux, and today it's listed on the National Register of Historic Places. The turnoff to Little Buckaroo Ranch Barn is located 1.5 miles south of Coyote Valley Trailhead (1 mile north of Onahu Trailhead). Follow the dirt road west to a small parking area, then walk across a small bridge over the Colorado River.

Harbison Meadows

Enjoy a picnic lunch at Harbison Meadows Picnic Pavilion, located just north of Grand Lake Entrance Station. The meadows are named after Annie and Kitty Harbison, two fiercely independent sisters who moved here in the late 1800s, homesteaded 360 acres, and established a successful dairy ranch. When Rocky Mountain National Park was established in 1915, the sisters refused to sell their land. In 1938, the Harbisons died a few days apart, and the park later acquired their property. The ranch buildings, including two cabins where the sisters lived, were removed in the 1970s to build Kawuneeche Visitor Center.

Kawuneeche Visitor Center

Located 0.4 miles south of Grand Lake Entrance Station, Kawuneeche Visitor Center has exhibits, an information desk, a store run by the nonprofit Rocky Mountain Conservancy, and a Wilderness Office (970-586-1242) where you can reserve and pick up backpacking permits. Perhaps most importantly, it also offers the park's only flush toilets west of the Continental Divide.

❧ ADAMS FALLS ❧

SUMMARY Adams Falls is a quick, easy hike to a lovely waterfall. Not surprisingly, it's one of the most popular trails on the west side of the park. Although most impressive in spring, when East Inlet Stream swells with snowmelt, it's also dazzling in late September when the surrounding aspen turn brilliant gold. From East Inlet Trailhead follow the trail 0.3 miles and turn right at the junction. Stone steps descend to a viewing area above the cascading waterfall. Adams Falls was named in 1917 after Jay Adams, a local resident who threw parties nearby. Its previous name, Ouzel Falls, came from American dippers (aka ouzels), which you can sometimes see plunging in and out of the water (p.91). After admiring the waterfall, follow the trail east above East Inlet Stream until it rejoins East Inlet Trail. Turning left takes you back to the trailhead. Consider turning right and hiking one mile farther to East Meadow, which some people consider prettier than Adams Falls.

TRAILHEAD (Elevation: 8400') East Inlet Trailhead is located near the end of West Portal Road, near the eastern end of Grand Lake.

◖ TRAIL INFO ◗

RATING Easy

HIKING TIME 1 hour

DISTANCE 1.1 miles, round-trip

ELEVATION CHANGE 97 feet

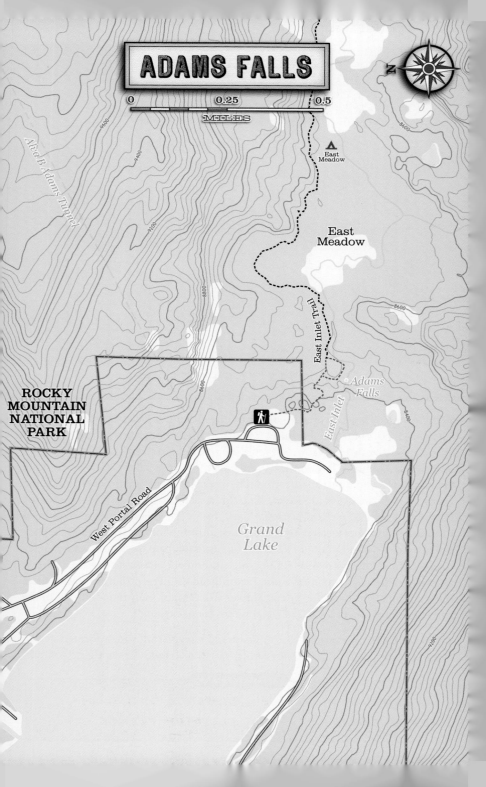

❧ LULU CITY ❧

SUMMARY This peaceful hike follows the Colorado River upstream to Lulu City (p.116), an abandoned mining town that briefly flourished in the late 1800s. This is the ultimate ghost town—even the buildings have vanished! Although it's still possible to find a few scattered remains, the hike to Lulu City is much more about the journey than the destination. This is a great way to experience the headwaters of the Colorado River, which starts its epic 1,500-mile journey to the Pacific in Rocky Mountain National Park. From the Colorado River Trailhead, hike north up a short, steep hill. You'll pass through forests and meadows, occasionally skirting the Colorado River as you head north up the Kawuneeche Valley. Keep your eyes out for wildlife. Deer, moose, and elk often graze in the lush surroundings. Roughly two miles from the trailhead you'll reach Shipler Park, where the log cabins of prospector Joseph Shipler still remain. Continue 1.5 miles to the pretty meadow where Lulu City's 40 buildings once stood.

TRAILHEAD (Elevation: 9,010') Colorado River Trailhead is located across from Timber Lake Trailhead, three miles north of Timber Creek Campground.

TRAIL INFO

RATING Moderate

HIKING TIME 5 hours

DISTANCE 7 miles, round-trip

ELEVATION CHANGE 482 feet

⊰ SHADOW MOUNTAIN ⊱

SUMMARY The first 1.5 miles of this hike is an easy stroll along the eastern shore of Shadow Mountain Lake. The next 3.3 miles climbs over 1,500 feet to a historic fire lookout tower near the summit of Shadow Mountain. From East Shore Trailhead follow East Shore Trail along Shadow Mountain Lake. Beyond the lake's northern shore you can see the Never Summer Mountains, birthplace of the Colorado River, which flows into the lake. At mile 1.5, two paths diverge into the woods. Bearing right takes you 1.3 miles to Shadow Mountain Dam. Bearing left takes you up the western flank of Shadow Mountain, which is covered in a cluttered forest of lodgepole pines devastated by beetle kill (p.77). Upon reaching the lookout tower you'll enjoy dramatic views of Grand Lake, Shadow Mountain Lake, and Lake Granby. The rustic three-story stone-and-wood tower was built in 1932 and occupied during fire season until 1968. Today it's the last surviving fire lookout tower in Rocky Mountain National Park.

TRAILHEAD (Elevation: 8440') East Shore Trailhead is located just south of the town of Grand Lake, off Jericho Road.

TRAIL INFO

RATING Strenuous	**DISTANCE** 9.6 miles, round-trip
HIKING TIME 4–5 hours	**ELEVATION CHANGE** 1,533 feet

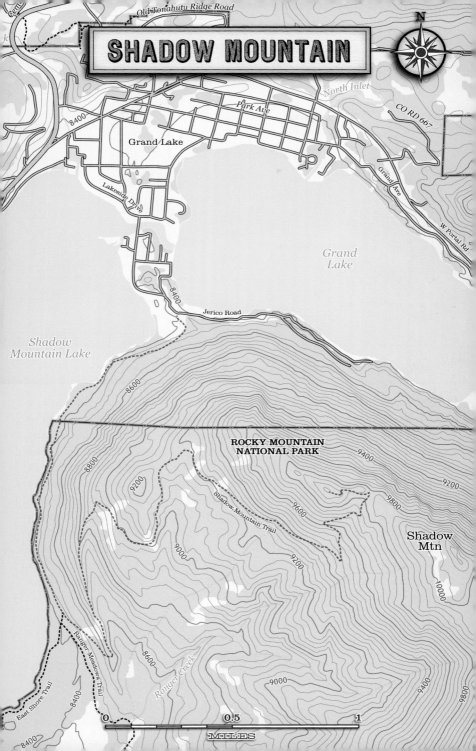

⤜ LAKE VERNA ⤛

SUMMARY One of the longest hikes on the west side of the park leads to one of its most stunning lakes. The trail to Lake Verna also includes easy hikes to Adams Falls (0.3 miles) and East Meadow (1.3 miles), plus a stenuous but slightly shorter hike to beautiful Lone Pine Lake (5 miles). From East Inlet Trailhead, hike to the junction to Adams Falls (p.280), bear left, and continue one mile to East Meadow. Elevated outcrops along the trail provide gorgeous views of East Inlet Stream as it gently twists through a lush meadow framed by distant peaks. The trail continues east, rising above the north side of the valley and offering glimpses of Grand Lake to the west. You'll climb impressive stone steps and cross rustic wooden bridges en route to Lone Pine Lake (elevation 9,894 feet), which is a great place to rest. Continue 1.9 miles to Lake Verna, where a distant ridge on the eastern horizon marks the Continental Divide. A beautiful sand beach covers Lake Verna's far eastern shore.

TRAILHEAD (Elevation: 8400') East Inlet Trailhead is located near the end of West Portal Road, near the eastern end of Grand Lake.

TRAIL INFO

RATING Strenuous	**DISTANCE** 13.8 miles, round-trip
HIKING TIME 9–10 hours	**ELEVATION CHANGE** 1,809 feet

⊲ TIMBER LAKE ⊳

SUMMARY This long, challenging hike leads to three beautiful lakes nestled in a dramatic valley. Looking for something easier? Hike 0.6 miles to Beaver Creek, where several pretty cascades tumble under a wooden footbridge. Timber Lake hikers push on, following the trail as it wraps around the southern flank of Jackstraw Mountain. This stretch is particularly lovely in autumn, when golden aspen light up the trail. About 2.5 miles past the trailhead the trail crosses an active landslide with loose footing. Before hiking, it's a good idea to inquire at a Wilderness Office about the current condition of this landslide, and use extreme caution if you decide to cross. Past Timber Creek Campsite (three miles), the trail parallels Timber Creek en route to a remote meadow frequented by elk and moose. A short side trail leads to a pit toilet. Beyond the meadow a set of switchbacks rises to Timber Lake's western shore, where the trail officially ends. Two smaller lakes are situated above Timber Lake.

TRAILHEAD (Elevation: 9,000') Timber Lake Trailhead is located three miles north of Timber Creek Campground.

TRAIL INFO

RATING Strenuous	**DISTANCE** 9.6 miles, round-trip
HIKING TIME 7–8 hours	**ELEVATION CHANGE** 2060 feet

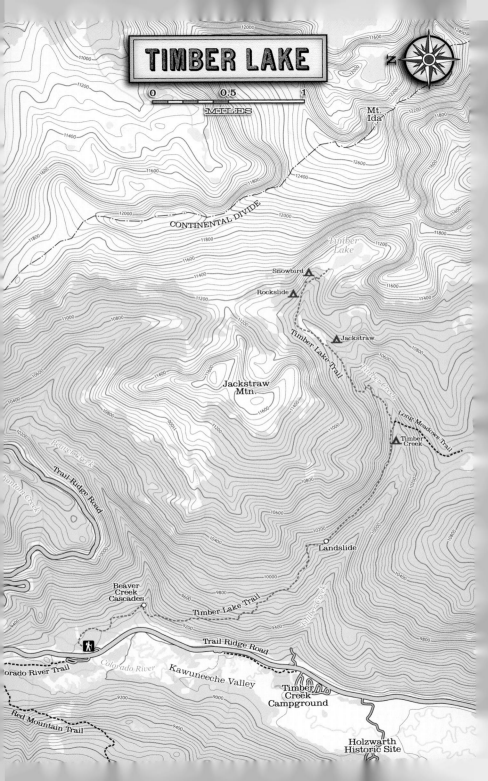

~⊰ CONTINENTAL DIVIDE ⊱~

SUMMARY This 26-mile loop—normally done as a multi-day backpacking trip (p.19)—rises nearly 4,000 feet to the Continental Divide. Sadly, many forested sections burned in the 2020 East Troublesome Fire. If you don't mind hiking through burned forest, you can still enjoy seven miles of spectacular views above treeline. Most hikers start Western Loop at Tonahutu Trailhead, following Tonahutu Creek and passing Granite Falls (7.5 miles) en route to campsites near the side trail to Haynach Lakes. Past Tonahutu Creek you'll rise above treeline into alpine tundra, entering Western Loop's most dramatic section, which offers gorgeous, panoramic views. Between Ptarmigan Pass and Flattop Mountain, the trail straddles the Continental Divide. During monsoon season, aim to be below treeline before afternoon thunderstorms hit. There are several wilderness campsites near the trail to Lake Nanita, which makes a terrific side trip. To finish the hike continue along North Inlet Trail to the North Inlet Trailhead.

TRAILHEAD (Elevation: 8,552') Tonahutu Trailhead is located just north of Grand Lake, off road 663. Park at North Inlet Trailhead, just up the road.

TRAIL INFO

RATING Strenuous	**DISTANCE** 25.8 miles, round-trip
HIKING TIME 2–3 days	**ELEVATION CHANGE** 3,721 feet

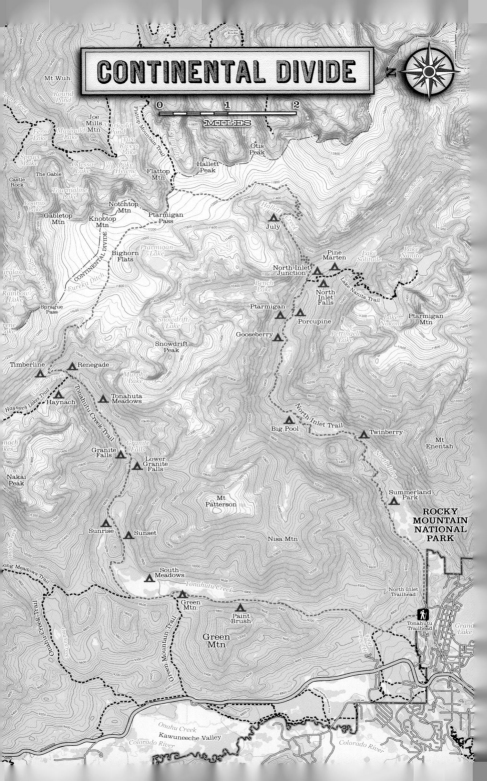

Extraordinary Guides to Extraordinary National Parks

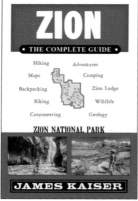

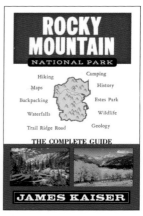

Travel tips, lodging info and more at
jameskaiser.com